Unwavering

The power of choice

Jen Baker

WAVERLEY ABBEY
RESOURCES

DEDICATION

To Nicole DeWard – a woman
of strength, wisdom, purity, faith,
boldness, and an unwavering desire to
live her best life, leaving a legacy for
thousands of others behind her.
I am so proud of you.

Contents

Part Three – Let's respond

Introduction

One of the most profound truths in the Bible is that regardless of how we came into this world – whether by love, passion or violence – we were chosen. God is intentional and at the moment of creation you were not only His first choice, but His best choice. At birth, He knew the number of hairs on your head (or lack thereof) and the number of days before you. God is responsible for bringing us into the world, but what we do with that time – and the legacy we choose to leave – is solely our responsibility.

Choice has existed since the beginning of creation. The first Hebrew word of the Bible means 'in the beginning' and the second means God (*Elohim*), with the third word, *bara*, meaning 'created'. Any type of creation, whether we are creating a meal or a memory, involves choice. Therefore, Elohim chose, before time was established, to express His love by appointing humankind as the recipient of His love; because love without an object to love is unfulfilled, empty and void of purpose. In other words, *you* are God's desire!

But you are a chosen race, a royal priesthood, a holy nation, a people for his own possession, that you may proclaim the excellencies of him who called you out of darkness into his marvellous light.
1 Peter 2:9

**Blessed be the God and Father of our Lord Jesus
Christ, who has blessed us in Christ with every
spiritual blessing in the heavenly places, even as he
chose us in him before the foundation of the world,
that we should be holy and blameless before him.**

Ephesians 1:3–4

As God's desire, and having been created in His image (Gen. 1:26), we carry His spiritual DNA, which means we also have the ability to choose, create and love. I believe that at the beginning of time God had dreams of His children multiplying in love, laugher, peace, joy, prosperity, influence and ownership. There are millions of stars and numerous planets… could it be that He originally created all of these for us to use, explore and enjoy?

Genesis 2:19 says that God brought the animals to Adam to see what he would name them. Adam did not have to prove his worth, take a course, finish secondary school or write a dissertation before he was given a responsibility which carried long-term influence. God is not a dictator who wants to control the universe, but a lover who longs to empower those He loves. He is far less concerned with our background and education than our willingness and obedience. Even Jesus chose 12 'working class' disciples… well, 11 of them came from Galilee and one of them was probably more educated than the others – Judas Iscariot. Education is important, but in the eyes of heaven it is not the only determining factor in who is qualified for service in the kingdom of God. With God, *all* are qualified – if they love Him and desire to obediently follow His lead.

When the Father asked Adam to name the animals, Adam

did not hesitate, ask for instructions, waffle about his inexperience or think of himself more highly than he ought... he simply obeyed. It is interesting to note that the first choice made by man was obedience, and the second quickly assumed leadership; unfortunately, what followed became an abdication of that responsibility. Gary Wiens speaks about those early days in his book *Come to Papa*, in which he says:

> *Satan's approach was to cause Adam and Eve to question what God really said, and his purpose was to bring doubt into their minds about the truth of God's attitudes toward them. They began to question whether God really had their best interests at heart. They wondered whether He would really satisfy their desires for significance, intimacy, and destiny. Satan appealed to their true sense of greatness, but he convinced them they they would need to grasp it themselves, instead of trusting the Father to give it to them by grace in the right time.*[1]

Once abdication occurred (which we will examine more closely later), fear had an open door through which to hijack peace and assume control. The more we allow fear and its friends a seat at the table of our heart and a voice at the seat of our consciousness, the less able we are to make choices based on kingdom principles. Living in a world saturated with entitlement-led thinking and victim mindsets has made choosing from a healthy, kingdom perspective increasingly more challenging, which is why I believe an unwavering lifestyle is non-negotiable for us as Christians.

Unwavering is divided into three parts and 12 chapters. Part One explores the power behind our choices and why it is vitally important to proactively take responsibility for those choices; Part Two identifies the faith and favour we have been given to fully embrace and live a kingdom lifestyle; and Part Three challenges us to intentionally develop a *momentum* of choice – giving us practical tools to make a lasting change.

My prayer is that as you read, fear will lose its grip, faith will come alive and purpose will be realigned… positioning you for a lifetime of relentless, kingdom pursuit.

This is your time, and this is your choice – make it an unwavering one.

PART ONE

Let's get ready

What went wrong?

Choosing from identity,
not insecurity

I never realised how blessed I was to grow up in mid-west Michigan, USA – a state known at that time for its cold winters and brutal blizzards (among other things). I wouldn't have wanted to be an adult during those snowstorms, navigating the closed roads and power outages, but as a child, the winter wonderlands created lifelong memories for me. Reminiscing about the Michigan winters conjures up images of snowdrifts, snow angels, snowball fights, snow dens... you get the idea, lots of snow! As kids, my sister and I would often play outside for hours (at least it felt like hours) until our faces were frozen, and then we'd waddle in our wet snowsuits back to the house for a hot chocolate. Sitting by the fireplace to thaw out, noses running, hair sticking out every which way from our woolly hats, eyes glistening with laughter at the fun we had... it all sounds rather idyllic looking back on it. But there was one particular winter that stands out above the rest, when we had the most devastating, and beautiful, winter storm that I can remember.

Our school had already been closed for a few days due to a blizzard when we heard news of an impending ice storm. My only thought was, *Yes! More school closures!* What we woke up to the next morning felt like a fairy tale. Living in the countryside meant we were surrounded by hundreds of trees, and each of these trees glistened like they were covered in diamonds, the winter sun reflecting from one icicle to the next, bouncing off each other like a visual symphony. It was simultaneously magical and breathtaking. I imagine if smartphones had been around at that time some of the pictures would have gone viral. Yet one of the downsides to this extraordinary beauty was that it froze the power lines and pipes, which meant no electricity or water… for a week.

Thankfully, my father is brilliant under these kinds of circumstances, and before we knew it he had us all camping in the lounge, fresh logs perpetually burning in the fireplace, Bunsen burner set up for cooking and games laid out for playing. He would go to check on the neighbours and make sure they were doing OK, and then came back to keep the home fires burning – literally. What could have been one of our worst family memories became one of our best. At least it did from our perspective as kids – my parents may remember this story a little differently!

Days went by in this enforced home-camping expedition, and soon the strange became the standard as we navigated bathing sparingly, eating differently and, if I remember rightly, melting snow for water. Finally, the day arrived when the power was restored and life went back to what we had known before our mini-Narnia experience. I was sad that the adventure was finished, but eager to step back into the twentieth century.

The day that I returned to my bedroom will forever be etched in my memory. During the deep freeze I had popped upstairs quickly to grab clothes, but it was far too cold to spend any time lingering up there. Now that the house had thawed, it was like arriving home after a holiday, putting things away and getting organised again. Suddenly I remembered something that my young, self-absorbed brain had forgotten all week: I owned a 113-litre fish tank, home to several fish, including my favourites as a pre-teen... the kissing fish.

Remembering that I was a pet owner brought me quickly back to reality. I hurried over to the area of my bedroom where I kept the tank, only to see my white kissing fish staring out of the glass, lips puckered, eyes bulging, as if they had been looking for me to rescue them, but, regrettably, were now... frozen solid. Oops! I removed the lid, only to discover it was a perfectly smooth ice rink fit for a mouse. The entire 113 litres of frozen water were essentially infused with motionless, aquatic corpses dotted throughout. My holiday, and my fish ownership, came to an abrupt end that day.

That fateful choice

Choices matter. We might expect children to be selfish when it comes to choosing – and my forgetting that I owned living creatures dependent on me for survival was not unusual for an immature girl obsessed with her own world. But as we mature, we are meant to think outside of ourselves, take responsibility for our purpose in this world, and leave a legacy for the next generation to build upon. We are all in this life together, 'Choices matter.' sharing the planet, living our dreams and desiring the best for ourselves, families and communities. Therefore, it is good to reflect on our own lives, looking at the choices we make to live this out in an intentional and proactive way. Are your decisions benefitting the greater community, as well as your own lifestyle? Despite what Simon and Garfunkel might say, we are not a rock, and certainly not an island; what we choose matters not only to us, but also to God's bigger picture.

As I said in the Introduction, I believe the Lord has had plans for His children that have never come to pass. We know Adam and Eve's story (Gen. 3:1–6), and people will forever reap the consequences of their fateful decision, one which catapulted humanity into a story of surviving instead of thriving. Once that door was opened, it could never be closed again. The choice was made and the repercussions were released: free will had spoken. Today that echo continues to reverberate in the millions of choices made by men and women around the world, each in their own way seeking to fill a void that Adam and Eve's foundational choice created.

How many times have we experienced an irreversible choice in our own lives – one much worse than killing a few fish – words we wish we could take back, actions that brought unwanted ramifications, thoughts which led us down a dark path toward an even darker behaviour? Thankfully, none of our choices had the catastrophic consequences of that first disobedient decision; nonetheless, any determination made out of flesh rather than spirit carries with it the potential for separation, with those around us and potentially with God. He will never leave us, but our closeness to Him can diminish over time.

Many years ago, at a time when I was struggling in life and consequently with God, I told Him that I did not care if He stayed or left – He could do whatever He wanted. I felt His presence hadn't exactly worked out too well for me up to that point, so what difference did it make? I was in a tremendous amount of hurt and confusion due to the hand life had dealt me and I was taking it out on the one that I loved the most, as humans normally do. After spouting my pity-filled response, I sensed the Lord take a gentle step back. He was not leaving, or even angry, but He was giving me space. It was like a veil had been pulled between us and He was leaving me to ponder my animosity. Our separation was not final, or even literal, but it felt like it at the time.

When we choose to ignore, reject, criticise, manipulate, wound and shame, our words are a greater reflection of the pain we are carrying then the object of our discontent. Blaming another person is always easier than looking at the source of our own hurt. We blame others for not meeting our standards, blame the government for the state of our country, blame leadership for disregarding our needs, blame God… for everything else! It is much easier to project blame than look at and take ownership of our own choices. Perhaps that's why both Adam and Eve shifted blame for the choices they made:

> 'Blaming another person is always easier than looking at the source of our own hurt.'

> **Then the man and his wife heard the sound of the LORD God as he was walking in the garden in the cool of the day, and they hid from the LORD God among the trees of the garden. But the LORD God called to the man, 'Where are you?'**
>
> **He answered, 'I heard you in the garden, and**

I was afraid because I was naked; so I hid.'

And he said, 'Who told you that you were naked?
Have you eaten from the tree that I commanded
you not to eat from?'

The man said, 'The woman you put here with me
– she gave me some fruit from the tree, and I ate it.'

Then the LORD God said to the woman, 'What is
this you have done?'

The woman said, 'The snake deceived me, and
I ate.'

Genesis 3:8–13, NIVUK

Can you relate? If something is not perfect in your world, do
you have a tendency to shift the blame off yourself and onto
someone else? I recently saw a brilliant quote on social media:
'Perfectionism is a megaphone of fear. Authenticity and trust are
our megaphone of faith. Let's make sure we are shouting the
right thing.'[1]

We will look at authenticity in more depth later, but now, at
the start of our journey, I would like you to think about what your
words tend to illicit – fear or faith? When Adam and Eve sinned,
God asked them where they were. He had not lost His children;
He was seeking honest, penitent hearts because He knows the first
step toward authentic freedom begins when we accept personal
responsibility.

A sign of the times

We cannot imitate the world and demonstrate the kingdom. As I write this, we have recently crossed into the year 2020 – not only a new year, but a new decade. While some people see no difference from one year to the next, or even one decade to the next, I believe there is tremendous significance in the kingdom of God with new seasons, years, decades and generations. God is not making it up as He goes along: He is strategically maturing His Bride (the Church) so she is ready for the outpouring of His presence and power, which will usher in a move of God that has been, until now, utterly unprecedented. I am not naming this as 'revival', 'the great revival', the 'end times' or anything else that would limit or box the concept. Regardless of what we call it, God still desires that every person comes to know Him, and the more we as a Church understand and practically demonstrate our identity in Christ, the faster I believe we will see this powerful move of God. Personally, I'm excited – and I want to be on the front lines of anything God is doing!

It is interesting to note that in Genesis 1, at the birth of humankind, we see an atmosphere shift instigated by God and experienced by humanity. Later, in Acts 2, at the birth of the Church, we see an atmosphere shift desired by 120 people and released by God. It could be argued that God instigated the Acts 2 outpouring as well, because He gave those in the upper room the desire to pray and seek Him, but they still had to choose. I believe a move of God follows a move of humanity, a move based on repeated choices to put Him first above any other desire. This is not a book on revival, and I am not remotely qualified to speak with authority on the subject, so understand that I am sharing what I sense in my spirit and see in Scripture.

In his brilliant book *The Burning Ones*, Steve Uppal says it this way:

> *This is not a move of God for leaders or to create a Christian elite. We will see people in everyday jobs and situations walking in the weighty, undeniable power of God. Some have referred to them as a nameless, faceless army, meaning that they won't be people with large churches, TV ministries or some great following. They will not be building a platform selfishly for themselves, but will point to Jesus in all things. He is turning His Body inside out and it is the day of the Church.*[2]

I'd like to add a loud *Amen* to Steve's words, especially as I too believe it is the time for us as the Church to be praying for and expecting this move of God. The early-nineteenth-century revivalist Charles Finney said, 'Prevailing prayer is that which secures an answer. Saying prayers is not offering prevailing prayer. The prevalence of prayer does not depend so much on quantity as on quality.'[3] We are not here to command God, but to work with Him; but in working with Him, we are to live and pray by faith, which is empowered by knowing our identity as seen by heaven.

In the upper room there were days of prayer and demonstrations of unity, and it was there that God poured out His Spirit powerfully. In 2 Chronicles 20 we see King Jehoshaphat facing a vast army ready to wipe out the people of Judah, and so he declares that all of Judah fast and seek the Lord – prayer, fasting, unity. In Judges 20 Israel was seeking to know if they should go into battle and once again they fasted, prayed and stood in unity (Judg. 20:11,26) until the battle was won. Before Jesus began His ministry He fasted, prayed and spent time in fellowship with His Father and Holy Spirit – prayer, fasting, unity.

Notice how, unlike society today, there was no victim mentality or self-pity response in any of these examples. They each knew their identity as a people chosen by God – quite simply, they trusted His sovereignty.

Testing and training

When we do not know our identity, we will attempt to create an identity in order to feel like we have an identity – and this will, at times, lead to turmoil and confusion. Alternatively, the more confident we are in our identity, the more at peace we will be with our decisions. I recently listened to a podcast where former astronaut Scott Parazynski was being interviewed about his life. He has accomplished five space shuttle missions and seven space walks, one of which included an extremely dangerous, never-done-before repair of a live solar panel. As Parazynski was explaining the rigorous training he had undergone to become ready for space, he said (and I am paraphrasing here):

'the more confident we are in our identity, the more at peace we will be with our decisions.'

'We know our role as astronauts, therefore NASA will try to kill you a hundred ways in the simulator... so that you will be ready for any emergency when you are up in space.' In other words, the purpose behind the pressure is, ultimately, protection. They are being rigorously trained so the mission will be safely accomplished – for them personally and for the entire team. When they are a few hundred miles away from Earth and the nearest B&Q, the astronauts need to know they are able to perform well under pressure without falling apart. Knowing they have been scrutinised under training conditions gives them the confidence to make life-changing decisions – which might have to be made in a matter of seconds.

As I was listening to this podcast I thought of the testing and training the Lord allows to happen in our lives. God does not cause or create our trials – He does not need to, since the enemy will make sure there are ample opportunities for us to be tested! But our loving Father uses what is thrown at us to strengthen us, for our future purpose and His future plans. Astronauts can confidently believe themselves to be adept in space because of their selection to the team, and the exhaustive training they endure. In the same way, we are accepted as children of God the moment we choose to follow Christ, but to gain the victory Jesus died to give us requires continuous training – and most of that training involves choosing our mindset and intentionally living out of our identity.

Do you know who you are?

If Adam and Eve had really understood that they were created in God's image, the temptation 'to be like God' would have not been a very effective temptation. Because they did not know or understand their full identity, they were susceptible to a lie disguised as an opportunity. We see this happening throughout the world today: there are so many people searching for meaning and living with an underlying fear that their identity as a wife/ husband, mother/father, sibling/child, friend, lover, employee, boss, leader will be removed from them... and then, without that role, who would they be? Without wearing a 'title', many of us feel uncovered and vulnerable, uncertain of where we belong and the part that we play in life. Gary Weins, in his book *Come to Papa*, says:

> *In our brokenness, in our fallen state, we fix our eyes horizontally, searching for some way to gain meaning in our lives. We look to human relationships, to the workplace, the sporting arena, the human leaders who are over us in order to try to fill the longing in our hearts for significance and destiny. We are particularly bent toward our own parents, and especially our fathers, who in their brokenness cannot fulfill that for which our hearts crave. Hear this now – they not only do not fill that place, they cannot... The yearning that exists inside the human heart has a God-shape to it, and only the Father of glory can release to us the reality that gives our lives their fullness.*[4]

A few years ago I read in the news about a man living in The Netherlands who decided that he wanted to legally be recognised as a 49-year-old, instead of his real age as a 69-year-old. He decided that because he felt like he was in his late forties (and, in his opinion, had the body of a 49-year-old) then he should have a right to legally change his age. His underlying reason, which he finally admitted, was to begin dating women 20 years younger than him. I'm not sure that lying about your age by 20 years is a particularly solid basis on which to start a relationship...

I'll be honest – I was gobsmacked when I read that. Of *course* you can't change your birth certificate to a different age simply because you feel younger! This man was, as a matter of biological fact, nearing his seventieth birthday... whether he liked it or not. His might be quite a bizarre case, but it clearly shows how a person who cannot accept their identity will try to create one they feel comfortable with – even if that identity is clearly fabricated.

Like I said, Adam and Eve were *already* created in God's image, but not recognising the power of that identity unleashed a sequence of events which continues to ensnare millions of people today. When we envy others, compare ourselves with those ahead of us (or behind) and judge what we may have never experienced ourselves, we set ourselves up for a colossal fall within the kingdom of God.

In a world that is saturated with subtle (and not so subtle) class systems, prejudice, mockery, injustice and elitism, we have a responsibility to live differently. Jesus knew His identity, therefore He never worried about His popularity, regardless of how many people misunderstood. His purpose would be fulfilled whether the people loved or accepted Him or not. Can we say the same?

Taking ownership

I was recently mentoring a lady through Coffee with Jen,[5] and while praying for her I had a picture come to mind of her on a horse holding a sword and a sceptre. I felt that the sword represented the Word of God, and the sceptre represented the authority of the kingdom. I sensed that this woman had used the sword powerfully in the past, but it was a season for the sceptre to rise up. In other words, time for her to walk in her God-given authority at a new level. She had been a seasoned Christian, intercessor and minister of the gospel for many years, but God was showing her that an upgrade was imminent.

Maturity brings upgrade, in the natural and in the spiritual. As we take ownership of our relationship with God and our identity in Christ, there is unlimited potential to serve others and to experience God's kingdom, outworked through our areas of influence. It would be foolish to expect promotion at our jobs if we never displayed greater skill, awareness, maturity or passion for our work. I was out to dinner with my parents a few months ago and it was evident that the waitress was not happy to be working on a Monday night. Her demeanour, tone and lack of enthusiasm showed us that she would have preferred to be anywhere other than serving us. Attitude is important and her ambivalent behaviour would never have secured her a promotion if I was her manager.

Even if we are not currently in our dream job, a kingdom lifestyle stays the course, gives with excellence, serves others

> 'Maturity brings upgrade, in the natural and in the spiritual.'

and always seeks to learn more in order to lead better. If you are leading a team of any kind, look for attitude and enthusiasm more than skill and proficiency – the latter can be taught, but the former can only be caught. Though we do not earn God's love or favour, we can earn promotion in the kingdom. As we mature, grow, learn, serve, walk in obedience and adjust our attitude, God notices and responds through expanding our territory and increasing our influence.

David killed the lion and bear when nobody knew who he was; nobody was watching to see if he protected his sheep; nobody cared that he went the extra mile; and nobody noticed when he arrived at the fields... nobody but God. He noticed. Therefore, when it came time to promote someone to become king, He remembered David, a man after His own heart (1 Sam. 13:14). Like Jesus, David was not swayed by the opinion of others, which is clear in how he handled the jealousy of his brothers:

> And David said to the men who stood by him, 'What shall be done for the man who kills this Philistine and takes away the reproach from Israel? For who is this uncircumcised Philistine, that he should defy the armies of the living God?' And the people answered him in the same way, 'So shall it be done to the man who kills him.' Now Eliab his oldest brother heard when he spoke to the men. And Eliab's anger was kindled against David, and he said, 'Why have you come down? And with whom have you left those few sheep in the wilderness? I know your presumption and the evil of your heart,

**for you have come down to see the battle.' And
David said, 'What have I done now? Was it not but
a word?' And *he turned away from him* towards
another, and spoke in the same way, and the people
answered him again as before.**

1 Samuel 17:26–30 (emphasis mine)

David turned away from the negativity, jealousy and criticism
of his older brother and turned toward one who would give him
the space he needed to step into his upgrade. If people around
you – even your own family – will not give you freedom to grow,
change and mature into your purpose and calling, then turn to
those who will. We are not obligated to remain under criticism
and negativity; the choice to walk away may not be ours, but
we can turn away, refusing to hear what has not been spoken
from heaven.

David's brothers felt entitled to their role in the battle, but the
fight was not won by entitlement; it was won by confidence, skill,
choice, and ultimately the grace of God. It was won by a young
man who was secure in his identity and known by his God. If you
find yourself sidelined and being unfairly treated, let the Spirit
direct your next steps. This season may have more to do with
your future upgrade than your current rejection.

'This season may
have more to do
with your future
upgrade than your
current rejection.'

When given the choice, Adam and
Eve chose insecurity over identity and
fear over faith.

In a world fuelled by blame, where
people incessantly shout 'rights' every

time there is a denial or disagreement, perhaps we could be more like David. He could have claimed his right to the kingdom after being anointed king, but he chose to wait for God's timing, and it was through that season of waiting that he developed the skill for slaying, which ultimately set him up for promotion. A promotion from heaven and not of himself – fuelled by blessing and not from boasting – one suited to a teenager slightly less self-obsessed than I was, who defends his animals… instead of deep-freezing them.

QUESTIONS

1. How would you describe your identity in Christ; what does that phrase mean to you?

2. Do you tend to blame others, or take on blame that is not yours? Does this change with your environment (at work, with family, friends, etc.)?

3. What does 'demonstrating the kingdom' mean to you?

Who is right?

Choosing to serve, not be served

I will greatly rejoice in the LORD; my soul shall exult in my God, for he has clothed me with the garments of salvation; he has covered me with the robe of righteousness, as a bridegroom decks himself like a priest with a beautiful headdress, and as a bride adorns herself with her jewels.

Isaiah 61:10

In God's kingdom royalty does not equal entitlement, it resembles servanthood. Being clothed with salvation and covered with righteousness carries a unique responsibility: this clothing is not only something we wear, it represents who we are. Righteousness does not give us permission to boast (we did nothing to earn these robes – see 2 Cor. 5:21), nor should it cause us to hide. Imagine if the Queen on her coronation had worn a ripped jumper or grubby t-shirt as she walked down the aisle to be crowned Queen Elizabeth II. The watching world would have been appalled! Of course she would never have worn anything less than grand because she is royalty, and as such, wears clothing worthy of that identity.

> 'In God's kingdom royalty does not equal entitlement, it resembles servanthood.'

At the same time, she did nothing to earn that royal title except be born 'for such a time as this', which, incidentally, is something we could all say about our status in the kingdom of God:

> **But you are a chosen race, a royal priesthood, a
> holy nation, a people for his own possession, that
> you may proclaim the excellencies of him who
> called you out of darkness into his marvelous light.**
> *1 Peter 2:9*

> **You shall be a crown of beauty in the hand of the
> LORD, and a royal diadem in the hand of your God.**
> *Isaiah 62:3*

> **[Jesus] made us a kingdom, priests to his God and
> Father, to him be glory and dominion forever and
> ever. Amen.**
> *Revelation 1:6*

Our spiritual clothing matches our identity, calling, purpose and destiny. Nobody in heaven is walking around in dirty rags or eating leftovers from the bin. There is no darkness, rubbish, crude graffiti or pollution; poverty, sickness, disease, greed and lack have all been refused entry into our heavenly home. In contrast, heaven is filled with gold, beauty, jewels, abundance, laughter, joy, pleasure, love… a home fit for the King of all kings *and* for us, His children. We read in John 10:10: 'The thief comes only to steal and kill and destroy. I came that they may have life and have it abundantly.'

God desires our lives to be characterised by abundance, but the one walking in wisdom allows God, not the world, to define what that abundance looks like and how it is distributed.

Bill Johnson sums this up beautifully by saying, 'Royalty is my identity. Servanthood is my assignment. Intimacy with God is my life source.'[6] We are royal, but that gives us the freedom to serve, not be served. That service can only be healthy and ongoing when it is fuelled by our intimate relationship with God, otherwise we can easily fall into one of the most common traps of our day: entitlement.

Entitlement

The book of Joshua provides an excellent example of entitlement leading to destruction. After 40 years of wandering around the desert, Joshua had finally led the Israelites into the Promised Land – arriving at the land they had dreamed of seeing all their lives. After years of toil, trouble, lack (in variety), and monotony, their lives had moved to a whole new level of blessing and bounty. They knew this was their season to live as their fathers had only dreamed of, and talked about, for years.

Imagine the excitement as the day arrived for their inauguration into their new homeland. Together this group of millions had already survived: death of their loved ones, wilderness, crossing the Jordan River, adult circumcision (all the men), eating manna for 40 years, silently marching around a city for six days... and now, after all of that waiting, obeying, sacrificing and anticipating, the day had arrived when they could finally shout and enter into their long-anticipated next season. All they had ever known led them to this moment when their legacy would no longer be defined by wilderness. But this promise arrived with a warning label attached: 'Do not to take any of the devoted things, as the treasure is meant for the Lord alone' (See Josh. 6:18–19).

> **On the seventh day, they got up at daybreak and marched round the city seven times in the same manner, except that on that day they circled the city seven times. The seventh time round, when the priests sounded the trumpet blast, Joshua commanded the army, 'Shout! For the LORD has given you the city! The city and all that is in it are to be devoted to the LORD. Only Rahab the prostitute and all who are with her in her house shall be spared, because she hid the spies we sent.** *But keep away from the devoted things, so that you will not bring about your own destruction by taking any of them.* **Otherwise you will make the camp of Israel liable to destruction and bring trouble on it.** *All the silver and gold and the articles of bronze and iron are sacred to the* **LORD** *and must go into his treasury.'***
>
> *Joshua 6:15–19,* NIVUK (emphases mine)

Outwardly it appeared that they had won the city for the Lord, but in chapter seven we get a glimpse into what really happened: 'But the Israelites were unfaithful in regard to the devoted things; Achan… took some of them. So the LORD's anger burned against Israel' (Josh. 7:1, NIVUK). At the next battle, instead of continuing on their winning streak, they lost 36 men and fear infiltrated the camp. Joshua was confused – and devastated – which altered his vocabulary from leader to victim. He said, 'Alas, Sovereign LORD, why did you ever bring this people across the Jordan to deliver us into the hands of the Amorites to destroy us? If only we had been content to stay on the other side of the Jordan!' (Josh. 7:7, NIVUK). The Lord was having none of that self-pity talk and immediately replied:

> **Stand up! What are you doing down on your face? Israel has sinned; they have violated my covenant, which I commanded them to keep. They have taken some of the devoted things; they have stolen, they have lied, they have put them with their own possessions. That is why the Israelites cannot stand against their enemies; they turn their backs and run because they have been made liable to destruction. I will not be with you anymore unless you destroy whatever among you is devoted to destruction.**
> *Joshua 7:10–12,* NIVUK

After some investigating, Joshua discovered that Achan was the one who coveted, and consequently sinned, by taking what was not rightfully his – leading to his death and the death of his family. Entitlement may feel good for a moment, but it always leaves destruction in its wake. We cannot sow selfishness and expect to reap blessing.

When we see our righteousness as something we are entitled to because of the blood of Jesus, or we believe that God owes us something because of all we have sacrificed for Him, it is greed and pride displayed in its rawest form. Let's not kid ourselves – we are not deserving of anything but death! In Romans 3:23 we read, 'all have sinned and fall short of the glory of God', and a few verses prior the apostle Paul says, 'None is righteous, no, not one; no one understands; no one seeks for God. All have turned aside; together they have become worthless; no one does good, not even one' (Rom. 3:10–12). The Bible is very clear that we have nothing to offer God but our sin, and to think otherwise is to tread upon the highway of arrogance... which is always located in the enemy's neighbourhood.

> 'We cannot sow selfishness and expect to reap blessing.'

Seeking to be served

In his 2013 TED Talk, psychologist Paul Piff explained how wealth can alter a person's levels of compassion and empathy. His research showed that as wealth increased, people's levels of compassion and empathy decreased, and their entitlement and ideology of self-interest increased.[7]

Let's be clear: wealth is not the antithesis of Christianity. Proverbs 10:22 says, 'The blessing of the LORD makes rich, and he adds no sorrow with it.' There are many examples of wealth in the Scriptures, including the book of Revelation, where heaven is described as being 'filled with jewels and beauty'. In addition, we know that Jesus had a bookkeeper to help keep track of the funds, and God did not ask Abraham to give away his money, but to sacrifice his son. The rich young ruler was challenged to give all of his possessions away because Jesus knew that money was his god and idolatry never brings true or long-lasting prosperity.

At the same time, wealth is not for us to accumulate and flaunt, but to use in serving others and furthering the kingdom of God. The Collins online dictionary describes entitlement as 'the right to have or do something'.[8] The sense of 'our right' is the feeling that we deserve something solely because of who we are. I remember visiting my father at his veterinary clinic when I was a teenager. I was proud of the fact that my dad was not only a vet but that he owned the clinic, and when I walked in I felt it was my right to have preferential treatment because I was 'the owner's daughter'. Well, Jesus was the Father's Son, but *He* never walked in entitlement! In fact, He came in the opposite spirit and honoured the one who gave the least over the one who gave the most (Mark 12:41–44). He let the prostitute kiss His feet, while rebuking the Pharisee for his arrogance (Luke 7:38–47). Jesus was God, and yet He honoured the government and paid His taxes in full, even inviting a tax collector into His intimate group of followers (Matt. 9:9). He never put Himself above the law because His focus was on serving, not benefitting.

We all will need to fight a sense of entitlement in our lives, especially in this day and age when it is becoming an epidemic to have our rights voiced and venerated. (To be clear, there *are* times to stand up for justice and truth, therefore it's helpful to ask if my motive is self-serving or God-honouring.) In the news recently, people were shocked to hear that a few celebrities felt it acceptable to illegally pay to get their children into prestigious universities. Unbeknown to the children, their parents paid thousands of dollars to ensure status was kept and appearance was maintained. It's easy for us to judge these parents, and perhaps be secretly pleased that the rich finally got caught in exploiting their riches, but before we throw the first stone it would be good to examine our own hearts. When have we stood in a supermarket queue feeling entitled to go before someone else because we only had a few groceries, or walked past a homeless person with even the mildest sense of 'better than'? When have we judged people in other countries for their poverty, or been annoyed at the driver in front of us keeping to the speed limit? Entitlement can creep into the smallest of spaces and purest of hearts if we are not mindful of its temptation. It is not restricted to the wealthy or unsaved; all of us have been tainted by a sense of 'deserving' over our lifetimes because it is rooted in sin, and we have all been born into the same sinful state.

There is not one person – rich or poor – more worthy than another for the blessed life Jesus died to give us. When I feel entitled to a specific type of service, position, respect, financial gain or possession, then I have forgotten that *God* is my source for every good gift (James 1:17). Am I saying that we have to forego any

'God's concern is not in the wealth we own, but when our trust in that wealth is greater than our trust in Him.'

desire to increase in position, finances, respect or possessions? Absolutely not! God's concern is not in the wealth we own, but when our trust in that wealth is greater than our trust in Him.

Let me be blunt – we will not sustain a life of peace if there is contention in our hearts between trusting God and a feeling that we merit blessings.

The gift of lack

I would not normally say that lack is a gift, but there are times when God uses what we do not have to reveal wealth we already possess.

When Adam and Eve felt deprived because something was being withheld from them, they did not realise it was actually God's protection. (As an aside, a God of love would never withhold out of cruelty – there is always a greater reason underpinning that decision, which may not be known to us this side of heaven.) When we choose to trust our questions to His love, we open the door to a greater revelation of His ways. Maturity happens when we do not need an answer from God, but instead rest in the knowledge that He is God… and that is enough. Adam and Eve learned that lesson the hard way, because they allowed their desire for more knowledge to eclipse the knowledge they already carried – His present and perfect love. They could not understand that what He sought to protect them from was a power they were not created to hold: to them it appeared that God was being selfish in His desire to keep the tree to Himself. Many times our seasons of lack can seem as if God is withholding something we desperately need – finances, breakthrough, spouse, children, job or a multitude of other desires. I have learned once lack becomes our focus then the desire to satisfy that void increases exponentially, and the enemy incessantly repeats, 'Did God really say…?', increasing anxiety and doubt in what was once a heart at peace.

Going without for a season reminds us – teaches us – that God is our ultimate source, and if we want to truly walk in freedom, this truth must be cemented stronger than our need for understanding. It is easy to say that God is our provider, until we lose our job, home, child, spouse or freedom. Then, who do we trust? Can we still say that our trust is in the Lord and He alone satisfies the deepest desires of our heart? I have learned to embrace those seasons as opportunities for growth and breakthrough, because once I can trust God with my emptiness, then I can start trusting Him with my questions. The more I can trust, the less I will fight; the less that I fight, the more freely I can receive. Finally, when I have arrived at that place, I realise that my peace is not based on the packaging in which the answer arrives, but the provider of that package.

'once I can trust God with my emptiness, then I can start trusting Him with my questions.'

There is a fine line between believing by faith that my healing, provision, blessing and salvation has been provided for me, and me telling God what to do. Was everything done at the cross? Yes. Does Jesus need to die again when a cancer diagnosis is given or a bill cannot be paid? No. Does this give me the right to dictate how and when that answer is to be provided? No. Are there times that His ways are higher than mine and His thoughts beyond what I can understand in that moment? Absolutely – yes. He is God and I am not.

The victim

As well as resisting a sense of entitlement, we need to be on our guard against a victim mentality. Victim thinking will never produce victorious living… ask me how I know! For too many years I lived as a victim: seeing the negative, seeking self-pity and looking for handouts. Perhaps it was the 'younger child syndrome', feeling I was not as good as my older sister, and assuming I needed a reason for people to notice me. Or perhaps it related to the abuse I had experienced in my childhood, which planted seeds of confusion, fear and unrest. Whatever the reason, I lived for years with an underlying melancholic, dramatic and depressive nature, which believed the only way to be seen was to be in need.

It reminds me of the man in John 5 at the pool of Bethesda. He had been in that condition for 38 years, waiting for someone to help him to the water where he could be healed. (Surely in 38 years he could have maneuvered his way toward the water, even if it meant edging out his fellow invalids with his elbows!) In John 5:7 he says, 'Sir, I have no one to put me into the pool when the water is stirred up, and while I am going another steps down before me.' Part of the reason I do not have a tremendous amount of sympathy for the man is because Jesus did not appear particularly interested in his excuses either. He does not address the man's dilemma, ask him how difficult it's been over the years or indulge any self-pity. Instead Jesus says, 'Get up, take up your bed, and walk' (v8). Instantly, the man was healed and 38 years of waiting came to a screeching halt. Now the man needed to take responsibility for his life, no longer dependent on others, but taking up his own mat he walked into a life of (potential) freedom and upgrade.

Catering to a 'lowest common denominator mindset' will never bring people into real freedom. I am not saying to throw out empathy or ignore the broken and hurting, nor am I saying to pressure someone into performance or to judge them into shame; but I am saying that if we allow a victim mindset to shape a society, we will unintentionally leave freedom out of reach. We cannot simultaneously be a victim and live in freedom.

The first verse of Jesus' mission statement is: 'The Spirit of the Lord is upon me, because he has anointed me to proclaim good news to the poor. He has sent me to proclaim liberty to the captives and recovering of sight to the blind, to set at liberty those who are oppressed' (Luke 4:18). Nowhere in that verse do we see a seat at the table for self-pity or a vacancy for victim thinking.

> 'We cannot simultaneously be a victim and live in freedom.'

Think about that practically – why would God want us to remain a victim when He *died* for our victory? Of course we need programmes to help people who are unable to make a different choice or who struggle mentally to break free of life-controlling issues or addictions. Of course we must *absolutely* meet people where they are at and give them the space they need to make the choices they want, but when the voice of truth is eclipsed by a display of pity then the Church has abdicated her position and responsibility to bring a kingdom atmosphere here to earth. It is a dangerous and slippery slope. The exciting news, I believe, is that we are positioned right now to hear a new sound arise from Christ's Bride... not the voice of a victim, but the harmony of love.

The power of love

A good question to protect ourselves from both entitlement and victim thinking is to ask: Would love make this choice? I realise it's not always cut and dry, and there are times when love makes a choice that might appear to be incompatible with Scripture (the main example being God giving His Son over to death). But love is still the best guide, as we can read in Colossians 3:14: 'Most of all, let love guide your life, for then the whole church will stay together in perfect harmony' (TLB).

> 'Would love make this choice?'

It seems that every day we have opportunities to practise this truth and yet, at least for me, it does not seem to get much easier! When have you chosen love over a fleshly response? How about when you know you are right about a disagreement, but choose to let the other person 'win' the argument; or when your teenager comes in after drinking, but love chooses to speak calmly to him in the morning; or when the tone of your spouse is not appropriate, but love remembers he is extremely stressed at work right now; or when you are in a rush and the teller moves as fast as a sloth, but love chooses not to tap her fingers as she waits? Before getting angry, judging, criticising, complaining or comparing, take a minute to consider love.

Not long ago I was around a group of people who were seriously challenging my patience, and I found myself quietly declaring 'love is patient' on repeat, while employing hidden deep breathing techniques to remain calm. Let's be honest – we do not always need to inform everyone how we are feeling, or make them aware of the stress they may be causing us at that moment.

Love them. Pray for them. Bless them. In the scheme of things, usually the situation does not merit anything more than that. I enjoy (and am often convicted) reading the famous 'love passage' from 1 Corinthians:

> Love endures long *and* is patient and kind; love never is envious *nor* boils over with jealousy, is not boastful *or* vainglorious, does not display itself haughtily. It is not conceited (arrogant and inflated with pride); it is not rude (unmannerly) *and* does not act unbecomingly. Love (God's love in us) does not insist on its own rights *or* its own way, *for* it is not self-seeking; it is not touchy *or* fretful *or* resentful; it takes no account of the evil done to it [it pays no attention to a suffered wrong]. It does not rejoice at injustice *and* unrighteousness, but rejoices when right *and* truth prevail. Love bears up under anything *and* everything that comes, is ever ready to believe the best of every person, its hopes are fadeless under all circumstances, and it endures everything [without weakening]. Love never fails [never fades out or becomes obsolete or comes to an end].
>
> *1 Corinthians 13:4–8,* AMPC

Fighting the entitlement spirit that is ravaging our world today will take a generation of people sold out for love: God's love for humankind and our love for God... therefore our love for humankind. Servanthood comes from love, protection arises out of love, generosity is born from love, and sacrifice shows the ultimate act of love. How are you doing in the areas of serving, protecting, giving and sacrificing for your neighbours, community and nation? Are you doing this through prayers (regardless of governmental leaders), volunteering and/or your occupation? I'll be honest, this is an area that I need to work on myself. Too often I am selfish, self-centred and focused on my own needs to think beyond *my* world to the needs in *the* world.

Love looks at others – it sees what entitlement is too proud to recognise, and fear is too selfish to explore. Pride and fear seduced Adam and Eve, but love found and set them free. Today, how can you display that same selfless love to those that you meet?

QUESTIONS

1. Have you ever felt that God owed you an answer to your prayer/question? How do you think He saw that situation?

2. When have you seen lack in an area turned into blessing?

3. When have you chosen to show love to someone who has hurt you, instead of choosing to be a victim of that hurt?

Why does this matter?

Choosing truth over sight

While scrolling through social media recently, I read a story that went something like this.

A woman on a sightseeing tour at Iceland's Eldgjá canyon was reported missing by her bus driver. The driver described the missing woman as 160cm tall, Asian and wearing dark clothing. A helicopter was sent by the coastguard to help search for the woman, while the rest of the tour group began to look for her on foot. About 50 people joined the search, including the 'missing' woman herself! What had happened was the woman had changed clothes and didn't recognise the description of herself. The search was called off at 3am, 'when it became clear the missing woman was, in fact, accounted for and searching for herself'.

After laughing at the ludicrousness of the story, it occurred to me that this is how so many of us in the Church are living today – looking for an identity which has already been found in Jesus. Too often we are striving to become something or someone we see emulated on social media, instead of sticking to the basics of loving God and loving people, as Jesus commanded us to (see Matt. 23:36–40). In my book *Unshakeable Confidence*, I say this:

> *Integrity has become a relative concept and personal 'rights' have become the popular platitude whenever someone acts in a manner*

that conflicts with our soul's comfort zone. Once God and His Word are removed, there is no truth – no basis on which to judge what is right or wrong.[9]

As long as we are looking for something more than what we find in the Gospels and through the shed blood of Jesus, we will be on an illusive, never-ending search, making choices based on fear instead of faith. In this day and age, it's important to not only know the Word, but believe the Word; not only know the Spirit, but let the Spirit move in and through our lives. I believe we have entered an era unlike any that we have seen before, and God is looking for people who walk in their God-given identity and are not ashamed to stand for truth and justice. These are exciting days. Can we put aside pre-conceived ideas of what God is going to do and simply open our hearts, hands and homes to what He chooses to do?

> 'God is looking for people who walk in their God-given identity and are not ashamed to stand for truth and justice.'

Abdication

According to the Merriam Webster online dictionary, abdication means 'an act of abandoning or discarding a right, responsibility, etc'.[10] One of the most famous abdications was by King Edward VIII, who gave up the crown in order to marry Wallis Simpson, a divorced American socialite, in 1936. History shifted significantly that day.

Thousands of years earlier, in the Garden of Eden, Adam and Eve abdicated their God-given responsibility. They had the right to everything in the Garden – they had rule over all of creation, the possibilities of their future and future generations was endless and infused with blessing – yet in one moment of abdication, they threw it away. All was now lost, and the keys to confusion, fear, death and the grave were replicated and released to every person born thereafter. They chose impulse over identity and the rest is history.

Fast-forward a few years and you'll meet Esau, who gave up his birthright because what he saw in the moment seemed more important than what he would receive in the future. I am not sure there is a more poignant example of how devastating it can be to live for today, forgetting about tomorrow, than this story:

> **Once when Jacob was cooking stew, Esau came in from the field, and he was exhausted. And Esau said to Jacob, 'Let me eat some of that red stew, for I am exhausted!' (Therefore his name was called Edom.) Jacob said, 'Sell me your birthright now.' Esau said, 'I am about to die; of what use is a birthright to me?' Jacob said, 'Swear to me now.' So he swore to him and sold his birthright to Jacob. Then Jacob gave Esau bread and lentil stew, and he ate and drank and rose and went his way. Thus Esau despised his birthright.**
>
> *Genesis 25:29–34*

Esau wasted a prosperous future in order to satisfy a present hunger. We may hold differing opinions as to whether King Edward VIII was right to give up the throne to satisfy the desires of his heart, but when it comes to spiritual abdication, history is quite clear on the dangers. Adam and Eve not only lost the right to walk in the Garden, but their relationship with the Father was never the same again. Selfishness never pays a reward worth keeping.

When we act out of selfishness, we may win the battle but still lose the war – so we need to ask ourselves if winning is really worth it. Does that person honestly need to know what I am thinking? Would love make that choice? Taking a step back and asking these questions may at the very least free us from the prideful snare of always needing the last word!

'Selfishness never pays a reward worth keeping.'

Another important point about a self-serving mindset is that it sometimes sneaks in the back door, so to speak, by masquerading as humility. For example, perhaps we have chosen inaction over confrontation, telling ourselves that it's to 'cover the other person', when really we are protecting ourselves from an awkward conversation. Sadly, I have a wealth of experience in this area; on more than one occasion I knew in my spirit that I needed to confront someone, but I abdicated my responsibility and chose an easier way out. The fear was too strong and my insecurity too great, so sheepishly I put self above the Spirit.

We might find it easy enough to imagine ourselves walking in courage and living like David, but when we are being mistreated it is much more challenging to rise above disparaging comments and speak the truth in love. (If you find yourself in any kind of abusive relationship, please speak to someone who can help. Do not try to fight this alone; you are much too valuable.) Regardless of how others treat us, the truth remains: God is our protector, defender and the one who defines our identity, value and worth – not other people. But while He is our defender, choosing how we respond is still *our* personal responsibility.

It's important we recognise this, because abdication always begins in the mind.

> 'choosing how we respond is still *our* personal responsibility.'

Moses must have watched the abuse of his people for years, thinking to himself that he would like to kill the Egyptians doing the abusing, until one day… he did. We do not suddenly wake up and decide to renounce our responsibility, leave our family, walk out on our job or quit the ministry. At the point of leaving, that decision has been ruminating in our minds for months, if not years. As I write this, the Duke and Duchess of Sussex have recently announced their plans to step down as senior members of the British royal family. They are not abdicating as such, but they desire to step back from royal duties and live a more 'normal' life as a family, including giving up their royal titles. It has caused quite a stir in the UK and around the world, with everyone watching to see Queen Elizabeth's response. So far, as I write, her response has been gracious and in keeping with unity, which not only doesn't surprise me, it encourages me. She sees the bigger picture and seems to be placing relationship above rule-following, or we could say grace over legalism. That grace allows her grandson and his wife to make decisions she may not agree with, but her love for them supersedes her control over them. It is a beautiful example of God's way with us. As much as God may want to protect us from dwelling on the negative and imagining the worst, He does not – because He has given us free will. Our abdication from believing truth never comes from heaven, but from our own desires becoming greater than God's timing and will for our lives.

One important distinction to consider is that God can separate us from adversity without telling us to abdicate our responsibility – and there is a difference. When we leave, as opposed to abdicate, we have time to prepare. Leaving involves having a conversation, and (hopefully) carries with it a process of putting things in place to protect those impacted by the decision. A season of preparation may not always be possible, especially if it requires agreement with others or when wrong is involved, but the heart of God would always lean toward unity. God's leading brings (inner) peace, purpose and protection, whereas abdication brings unrest, confusion and isolation. I have been involved in both sides and I assure you, God's way is *always* best. But for those times we choose unwisely (which we all do at times) there are, thankfully, several biblical examples of how we can navigate seasons of failure.

Failure

Having lived as a Christian for over 30 years now, I've had personal experiences with abdication, and the sense of failure in those situations was palpable. In some of those cases, I like to think I would make a different decision today – but I acted on what I felt was right at the time and with what information I held in that moment. It's worth considering that, at times, a decision may look like abdication, when in reality it's the bravest choice we could make. Life is too complicated to be written in black and white. But, if we're honest, occasionally we allow our flesh to speak the loudest, and end up making a rash decision in a heated moment.

That kind of behaviour reminds me of Peter, who seemed to have his foot in his mouth more often than on the ground! He was the one who rebuked Jesus (not his brightest moment), cut off a man's ear in anger, denied Christ, surrendered to legalism, left the guys alone to bring in the haul of fish, did not get along with John, tried to keep the children away from Jesus, interrupted a holy moment on the Mount of Transfiguration by asking if he should start a building project to honour that particular holy moment (again, not a bright spot in his story), slept throughout Jesus' deepest moment of need, and returned to fishing after Jesus had called him to disciple nations. Quite an epic list of failures to rack up in just three years! But I believe one reason we like Peter is the fact that we can identify with him – foibles and all. He made huge mistakes, but was teachable and would always return, willing to try again.

'Life is too complicated to be written in black and white.'

Failure is never final, unless we quit. Rather, failure is a gift which helps us decide how we want to live our lives moving forward. We can't take back what has been done, but we can change what is yet to come. I encourage you to never hide the shattered pieces of your story; instead, arrange them into a beautiful mosaic of a life fully lived. Once Peter stopped seeing himself through the filter of failure, and chose to believe his true identity, he stepped into the full authority of his purpose – and so can we.

> 'Failure is never final, unless we quit.'

A strong foundation

If abdication was the original downfall of Adam and Eve, and if we also find ourselves frequently making unwise choices, how can we live an unwavering lifestyle of faith when we are tempted in this area? The Bible says that perfect love casts out all fear (1 John 4:18) – love is always the answer. We have been created body, soul (mind, will, emotions) and spirit. Fear will often begin by tormenting our soul, which creates damage in our body, causing unrest in our spirit. Choosing to let our spirit take charge positions us for victory because God is love (1 John 4:16) and, ultimately, fear cannot stand against a power that strong.

Living without fear *is* possible when we place ourselves securely within the love of God. Imagine if we were to be spirit-led and not circumstance-driven in our decisions. Fear keeps us bound to our circumstances, but the Spirit keeps us linked to truth – only we can decide which one has the final word. With that in mind, I want us to finish this chapter exploring a verse that provides a brilliant foundation on which we can begin building a life of unwavering faith.

**For God has not given us a spirit of fear, but
of power and of love and of a sound mind.**
2 Timothy 1:7, NKJV

I was recently meditating on this verse when the Lord highlighted
to me some important keys. First, God does not want us holding
what He's asked us to leave. I realise this is perhaps easier said
than done, but fear *must* leave if we command it to go, because
we have authority over fear in Jesus Christ. This is not a time to
be half-hearted, but bold in our conviction –
slamming the door in fear's face! Acting in
this manner is an important first step, and
we need to understand this before moving
on. (Please note: There are times we need
someone else to pray with us and stand with
us to see fear go and peace come, so please do

> 'God does not
> want us holding
> what He's asked
> us to leave.'

not feel you must do this alone. We are the body of Christ for a
reason – we help one another in times of trouble, and this might
be a season to ask a friend to pray and stand with you in faith until
you experience breakthrough. Also, this may be a journey and not
happen immediately. God is patient and He will work with you
as you take steps toward freedom – there is no condemnation in
Him or from Him. The important thing to remember is that as a
believer in Christ, *you* are the one with authority – not fear. You
may want to continue reading and then return to this section later
to reinforce this truth.)[11]

Power

We have seen what God has *not* given, so let's focus now on what is ours to keep: power, love and a sound mind. The second key God revealed to me was that, in His kingdom, another word for power can be 'authority', and anyone who has authority will carry a level of power. That power and authority has, at times, been abused in the Church, but the principle remains the same: authority carries power. The Greek word for power in this verse is *dunamis*, which can be translated as 'miraculous power'. Every believer carries miraculous power by the Holy Spirit dwelling within them, and from the authority we have been given by Jesus Christ (see Matt. 28:16–20; 16:17–19). What a thought! We each have the ability to lay hands on people and see them healed, or speak words of deliverance over someone and see them set free. This is not only for preachers or the 'holy ones' but every believer in Christ.

I believe we are entering a season when this power and authority will be demonstrated on a scale we have not seen in this generation. No longer is this power reserved for the person up at the front, but it will flow through the neighbourhoods, cities, towns and across the country. We will see timid believers become bold, and those who have stood on the sidelines will step onto the front lines. It is a season when anyone who is hungry for God will be used by Him, and a time when dreams and prophetic words that we have held, perhaps for decades, will come to pass in a short amount of time. I believe we will be astounded at the speed with which this move of God happens and the vast influence of where it goes – we may be surprised at the people God chooses to use when it falls outside our religious paradigm of who is worthy in the kingdom. This is a time to set aside judgment and put down racial and denominational walls – unity is the calling card of the kingdom in this season. He has been preparing His Bride for years and the birth pangs are getting stronger, the defences of the enemy weaker and the veil between heaven and earth thinner. It is time to step up, speak up and show up. Not as a weak vessel, one easily moved by every trouble or disappointment, but as one ready to fight for truth and stand for justice. Heaven is helping us, and that will never change, but this is a season to be released into our personal Promised Land – no longer dependent on manna to survive, because we are fighting from the abundance that is ours to possess. What will be *your* role in this new season?

'It is time to step up, speak up and show up.'

Before you think that you have nothing to give, remember the time over five thousand hungry people needed to be fed, and Jesus told the disciples 'you feed them' (Matt 14:16, TLB). Many pastors or evangelists might feel that, as the leaders, *they* should be the ones who do the praying, but Jesus wanted to show the disciples that *they* carried the same ability to bring about a miracle. When they balked at the impossibility of feeding that many people, Jesus told them to take a stock inventory. After investigation they discovered five loaves of bread and two fish were all that was left. (As an aside, we always have *something* that can be used as a seed to sow for our needed miracle, no matter how small.) Jesus prayed, blessed the food, and then He *gave it to the disciples to distribute.* Notice that Jesus was not holding enough bread to feed the multitudes when He handed it to the disciples, and even the pieces He did have were broken down further. When we feel inadequate, powerless or that there isn't enough, the key decisions are: refuse fear, take ownership of the situation, look for an opportunity to give out of what we currently hold, obey… and then expect a miracle.

Agape love

Not only have we been given power, but we have also received love – agape love. Writing about love could be an entire book in itself, so in this limited space let's briefly explore how love affects our choices. The Greek word *agape* is divine love, as opposed to a love of flesh or friendship, and it is the deepest and purest form of love. As we saw earlier, God *is* love – and we are made in the image of God (Gen. 1:26) – therefore, love can also describe our identity. I am reinforcing this truth because, although we know this intellectually, most of us are not fully walking in this spiritually and emotionally. This identity of love is something we must continue meditating on to thoroughly receive its revelation, if that is even possible this side of heaven!

In his devotional *The Divine Romance*, Dr Brian Simmonds says it this way:

> *God Himself has pulled you into this never-ending, always-connected dance of love. It permeated you and embraces you with perfect harmony. Entwined within His presence, life takes on new meaning. Impossible situations become possible. Faith rises to an entirely new level. Joy overcomes sorrow, confidence replaces self-doubt, and love conquers fear.*[12]

How many of us wake up in the morning, intentionally viewing our lives from this perspective of an heir to the kingdom and a recipient of divine love? If I have to remind myself that I am royalty, then somewhere at its core my mindset is aligned with poverty thinking, because fruits reveal roots and actions reveal thoughts. If the Church does not understand or even believe her kingdom identity, then how can we expect anyone outside of a relationship with Christ to gain revelation, or even an interest, in what is freely available to them?

A sound mind

Actions based on authority and rooted in love are crucial to walking in biblical truth, but there is one vitally important area to guard if we want to be fully empowered to choose from identity and not from fear. The last part of that verse from 2 Timothy declares that we have been given a sound mind. As Jesus is the healer of our bodies, He is also the healer of our minds. Torment is never from heaven and anxiety cannot reign in a peace-filled heart. That being said, I understand that anxiety and fear are a genuine struggle for many people, especially in today's world. Hatred, fear, anger, abuse, criticism, bullying, demeaning, despair and much more have been released from the enemy, and unless we intentionally choose to stand against them, we may easily succumb. It is like going mud-wrestling and then getting annoyed when we come away caked in dirt – the only way to stay clean is to refuse to engage in the fight.

The world is ready to influence what we refuse to guard –

so we need to guard our minds! Imagine a holy Secret Service standing guard over your mind, eyes and ears… is there anything you are currently allowing to influence your life that they would say should have no access? Or have we given an 'all access pass' to whatever thoughts come to us, regardless of their origin? In the same way that a celebrity can overrule their protector's advice, you are the ruler of your own domain. But wisdom listens to the experts, and if the Holy Spirit senses trouble, we'd be wise to pay attention!

> 'The world is ready to influence what we refuse to guard'

Many years ago, when I was a teenager and not yet a Christian, I dabbled a bit with an Ouija board. I did not realise there was so much demonic power behind what seemed like just a bit fun at the time – but I was about to find out the truth. The enemy does not play games. It was around that time in my life when one night I saw a demonic presence at my window. I was absolutely frozen with panic – I literally could not move. In the midst of my terror I was able to boldly squeak out one word: *Jesus*. The moment I said His name, that spirit left and never returned. It was an experience I have never forgotten and it showed me at an early age the tremendous power in His beautiful name.

The last chapter of Mark's Gospel clearly shows us what the name of Jesus can do: empowering us to speak in new tongues, casting out demons and healing the sick. His name is the only name by which we can be saved, and at His name our enemy shudders. Perhaps we're so used to saying 'in the name of Jesus' at the end of our prayers that we have, at times, become immune to the power behind what we are saying. I know I can easily fall into that trap by finishing a prayer with that phrase, yet without any faith attached to what I am saying… the words just tumble out of my mouth along with the 'Amen'. Yet cancer can be destroyed in the name of Jesus, the deaf can hear, the dead can be raised, the minimum can be multiplied and the enemy can be defeated – *all by His name*! But if our minds are filled with confusion, fear, doubt, anxiety and unbelief, then we will find it extremely difficult to use His name with anything other than vain hope… hoping that something will happen, instead of knowing the truth will prevail. I lived that way most of my life and I refuse to do so any longer. Either God is God and has won the victory through Jesus, or not – and I believe that He has!

Changing mindsets is not a quick fix and can often take years as we establish new thought patterns, but change *is* possible. I explore this topic far more in my book *Unshakeable Confidence* and would recommend reading this book if this is an area of challenge.

And finally…

One day, while out for a morning run, I was listening to a podcast where a presenter used the phrase, 'the lifestyle we are accustomed to'. As he continued speaking, my mind began wandering and I started to consider, what lifestyle I am accustomed to? What things do I do or receive on a regular basis that make my life what it is, and how would I feel if those things were taken away? As I pondered these thoughts while pounding the pavement, the Holy Spirit interrupted my stride by saying, 'Jen: don't be concerned with the lifestyle that you are accustomed to, live the lifestyle you are called to'.

It occurred to me that the world sets a standard for itself, and most people try to achieve a level of contentment within that standard; that then becomes 'normal' and what they are accustomed to in their lives. In the kingdom we live by calling, not contentment, and our lifestyles should match the calling that is on our lives, as believers and as individuals. We are called to love our neighbour – that is non-negotiable as a believer. But each person also has a specific purpose for their lives, which God is asking them to live out through the different seasons.

'don't be concerned with the lifestyle that you are accustomed to, live the lifestyle you are called to.'

As I like to say, purpose is a journey, not a destination. We can get caught up in the idea of whether or not we have fulfilled our purpose, but I think following the leading of the Holy Spirit every day, living outside our comfort zone, walking according to the Word of God and keeping our hearts free from the world will automatically put us in line to walk out purpose, without needing to worry if purpose is being fulfilled. All of this happens to a greater degree once we decide to live by faith (truth) and not by sight (2 Cor. 5:7). So let me ask you: Are you ready to step into the life you were called to?

QUESTIONS

1. Do you agree with the statement 'abdication begins in the mind'? If so, how are you intentionally guarding your mind in this season?

2. What would forgiving yourself look like today?

3. What lifestyle has God called you to, and are you fully living in it?

Where to begin?

Choosing future reward over present regret

Have you ever faced a disappointment in life? If you have lived longer than a day, I am pretty sure the answer will be yes. We all face disappointments, hurts, rejection, let-downs, failures and regrets... they all form parts of our life's mosaic. Mosaics can be described as 'something beautiful created from something broken', formed by a creative process that requires intention, vision and patience. Often, the road back toward beautiful – after we have been broken – requires us to intentionally re-engage with an environment in which we have been hurt before, while trusting again... both of which are challenging at best and terrifying at worst. Have you ever noticed that disappointment will often lessen our future dreaming? We are afraid to dream because we can't face the idea of experiencing hurt and heartbreak once again, but we forget that having gone through that pain means that we are not the same person as we were before it. Choosing to learn from all our experiences – especially the painful ones – provides a measure of wisdom, strengthening our character and deepening our faith, while accepting that we may never fully understand why some things have happened in our lives.

Every day, we have the opportunity to forge new paths by making different decisions. You may have been stuck in a particular mindset for years, but today that can begin to change.

Throughout my years of being in ministry, I've had my fair share of failures: projects that did not take off, preaches that did not land, ideas that failed to flourish and decisions that not only hurt me but, tragically, also hurt people that I loved. Fear of offending created a fear of failure, which culminated in a fear of trying. It was a dangerous mountain to keep circling, and after one particularly difficult season, I decided that I had had enough of that kind of scenery: I was forging a new path from that day on. That one decision has literally changed my life, and it can do the same for you.

> 'Every day, we have the opportunity to forge new paths by making different decisions.'

I want us to briefly look at another colossal failure, in many respects; a man who decided that enough was enough, and chose to forge a new path.

Finish line or starting line?

When I was primary school age I was asked about my favourite Bible story, and the only one I could think of at that moment was the story about a little guy up a tree, who then ended up having Jesus round for dinner. The priest doing the questioning asked me why it was a favourite, and I turned bright red as I couldn't think of any reason – I just liked the idea of a short man being up a tree!

We know this 'little man' as Zacchaeus, a tax collector whom Jesus picked out of a crowd (or, ahem… a tree), and then preceded to invite Himself over to this 'sinner's house' for a meal.

Zacchaeus had deceived, stolen, cheated and probably lied to many throughout his life, and yet he was Jesus' chosen dinner guest. (I have to admit feeling challenged by this when I reflect on the last few dinner guests that I have invited to share a meal with me.) But despite all his past sin and manipulation, Zacchaeus was set free to start living a new life. Our past failures pale in comparison to the promise held for us in the future; rewriting history may not be an option, but our future is scripted through the pen we now hold. Jesus did not force Zacchaeus to accept His invitation and, similarly, God will not force us to make a new choice.

> 'rewriting history may not be an option, but our future is scripted through the pen we now hold.'

If the last chapter in your life is not a storyline you want to continue, perhaps it is time to write a new script?

Many people see failure as the finish line, when in reality it can become the birthplace of new beginnings and fresh vision. As I keep emphasising: if one choice has not worked, make a new one. I am not making light of devastating loss; every loss is a painful one when heart and soul have been invested into a relationship or season of time. But regretting what has happened, or refusing to let go of the pain, will not change the situation – and establishing a home around that hurt simply locks in what needs to move out. Only by looking forward, and making brave choices from the broken pieces, can we grow from our past pain.

Today, will you say 'yes' to handing the Father your brokenness… watching Him create something beautiful for you, and future generations, to gaze upon? If so, please take a minute to pause and reflect, then – before reading any further – pray this simple prayer with me:

Father, thank You for Your love for me, even when I feel unloveable. You know every detail of my life – the pleasant and the painful – and I choose today to hand You the shattered pieces. Please make something beautiful out of something broken. I put my hand in Yours and I invite you into the home of my heart, as Zacchaeus welcomed you into his story. Thank You for going on this journey with me. Amen.

An easy life

When we live a life surrendered to Christ we will have moments of unbridled joy, but equally moments of challenge and sorrow. In John 16:33, Jesus said: 'I have said these things to you, that in me you may have peace. In the world you will have tribulation. But take heart; I have overcome the world.' We cannot be involved in a spiritual war without facing a battle – not only is that impossible, it is presumptuous. Imagine if a new recruit arrives at boot camp only to tell her commanding officer that she is happy to learn how to fight, but she prefers not to travel with the squad to war. She would

'When we live a life surrendered to Christ we will have moments of unbridled joy, but equally moments of challenge and sorrow.'

find herself on the first flight home! Battle involves fighting, in the natural and especially in the spiritual. This is not something to fear, because we have been given the armour we need (Eph. 6), and a weapon (the Bible), a double-edged sword, by which we know that we have already won, yet we are still required to displace the enemy from trespassing on God's property.

Remembering that we do not battle alone is critical to our peace here on earth. In heaven there is perfect peace, and in Isaiah we are told that the Lord will 'keep him in perfect peace whose mind is stayed on [Him] because he trusts in [Him]' (Isa. 26:3). If we keep our eyes fixed on Jesus and we remain in a place of trust, that peace can also be ours here on earth. The word 'mind' in this passage is the Hebrew word *yetser*, which has several meanings: frame of mind; a focused mindset fashioning an overall strategic plan; anything that is formed or made and then refers to imaginations, thoughts or devices. Not only that, but the word 'stayed' is *samak*, and can mean: rest, support or sustain.[13] Therefore, I believe that if a mindset which frames what we believe and fashions what we see is resting on and supported by the Lord, then we can maintain peace, or *shalom* – God's gift of wholeness.

It is important to remember that peace which comes from heaven is not only available during our good seasons. God's peace, which passes all understanding, also exists in the challenging times. Often in the past I have used my circumstances as an excuse to dismiss what heaven was offering, but once I took my eyes off the pain and put them firmly on Christ I began to experience what seemed unexplainable: perfect peace. We read in the next verse of Isaiah 26: 'Trust in the LORD for ever, for

the LORD GOD is an everlasting rock.' This leaves no question
of Isaiah's directive for maintaining peace: we are to put our
absolute trust firmly in the Prince of Peace, who is immovable,
regardless of our circumstances.

Equally, if we choose not to place our minds on the Lord,
then we cannot blame Him for the consequences we might reap.
The late evangelist Reinhard Bonnke was once asked by reporters
how a good God could allow so much suffering in the world. He
said this:

> *You could just as well ask the U.S. Secretary of Transportation
> why he allows accidents on the highways. No doubt, he would
> take exception to your accusation, and point to the rules of the road.
> 'Every time a law is broken, an accident and suffering might occur,'
> he would reply.*[14]

Bonnke then went on to explain that when we break God's
'rulebook', there are consequences to those actions. Sometimes
it is society, and not us personally, that makes bad choices we
have no control over, which affects our lives. At such times, Isaiah
26:3–4 becomes paramount for us as we put our trust in God,
and not in the world, to bring us peace. By not knowing what is
rightfully ours to believe, we can miss what is rightfully ours to
own… satisfying ourselves with loose change when God wants to
give us a grand inheritance. God will not choose for us: it is our
responsibility to take our thoughts captive and let them rest on the
goodness, grace and greatness of our God.

He alone is perfect, He alone is worthy and He alone can
redeem any and all situations we face, if we choose not to give in

when it seems daunting to move on. Unfortunately, that choice was all too much for our next Bible character…

Saul

Fairly recently, it seems we have seen an increase in the number of famous musicians taking a public stand for Christianity, which has ruffled the feathers of some religious people who do not like the fact that a person's high-profile and somewhat chequered past could be washed away so quickly. If the blood of Jesus was not for people steeped in sin, then who was it for? Certainly not for the one so perfect that there is no need for a Saviour. Yes, we are called to pursue a life of holiness, and yes, our aim is to allow the love of God to transform us into the image of God. But we are also a work in progress, and if we do not allow ourselves (and others) the chance to grow, then we are no better than the Pharisees who wanted to stone the sinner and crucify the Saviour.

So let's take a look at one man in the Bible who, unlike these celebrities, refused to learn from his failure, put aside his pride or face his fears – choices which ultimately cost him his life. There are many lessons we can learn from Saul in the Old Testament, but let's first remind ourselves of how he began his leadership by looking at a few scriptures.

> **There was a man of Benjamin whose name was Kish, the son of Abiel, son of Zeror, son of Becorath, son of Aphiah, a Benjaminite, a man of wealth. And he had a son whose name was Saul,**

a handsome young man. There was not a man among the people of Israel more handsome than he. From his shoulders upwards he was taller than any of the people.
1 Samuel 9:1–2

Samuel answered Saul, 'I am the seer. Go up before me to the high place, for today you shall eat with me, and in the morning I will let you go and will tell you all that is on your mind. As for your donkeys that were lost three days ago, do not set your mind on them, for they have been found. And for whom is all that is desirable in Israel? Is it not for you and for all your father's house?' Saul answered, 'Am I not a Benjaminite, *from the least of the tribes of Israel? And is not my clan the humblest of all the clans of the tribe of Benjamin?* Why then have you spoken to me in this way?'
1 Samuel 9:19–21 (emphasis mine)

When he turned his back to leave Samuel, God gave him another heart. And all these signs came to pass that day.
1 Samuel 10:9

From the first encounter between Samuel the prophet and Saul the future king, we see identity – and insecurity – playing a headlining role in the dialogue. Though Saul was handsome, wealthy and physically built as a leader, he could not see beyond his upbringing… he was born into the clan of the Benjaminites. As the smallest of the clans (Benjamin was the last son of Jacob, whose sons became the leaders of the 12 tribes of Israel), Saul also defined himself as small – clearly unable to see beyond his birthplace. Too many people allow where they started to define where they finish. You could have been born on a council estate or in a palace, had absentee parents or looked for love in many wrong places… this does not define your future, it only explains your past.

Ironically, the words Moses spoke over the tribe of Benjamin were the following: '[You are] GOD's beloved; GOD's permanent residence. Encircled by GOD all day long, within whom GOD is at home' (Deut. 33:12, *The Message*). The promise was permanent residency by an ever-loving God, but Saul still chose to see the outward definition of his upbringing, rather than God's declared promise over their lives. Let's be careful not to make the same mistake. God's promise always trumps our past.

Saul's response to Samuel showed the power of insecurity, because he had everything that the world looks for in a leader – height, good looks, wealth – but, as a prophet, Samuel saw beyond the mirage to the mess that was inside of Saul. Despite Saul's fears, God's grace stepped in and gave Saul 'another heart'. In other words, even though an earthly king was not God's desire (1 Sam. 8:9), His love still empowered Saul to become the leader the people wanted.

> 'God's promise always trumps our past.'

Sadly, the assistance of heaven was still not enough to change Saul's behaviour. Saul's life shows us that God can give us a new heart, but if we refuse to adjust our beliefs and behaviour, then the new heart will eventually revert to its old, comfortable pattern of living.

In a nutshell, Saul was too distracted about where he had come from to understand what he had been given – his insecurity overshadowed his influence, leaving space for David to take his place (which we will read about later).

Hiding among baggage

So they enquired again of the LORD, 'Is there a man still to come?' and the LORD said, 'Behold, he has *hidden himself among the baggage.'*
1 Samuel 10:22 (emphasis mine)

Saul had recently been anointed king by the prophet Samuel, and now he was about to be crowned king in front of the people. Everyone was assembled together waiting to see which strong man of God would lead them into their next season. I can imagine the palpable excitement in the air, the special foods that may have been cooked for the occasion, the murmuring of gossip about who it will be, the young people excited for a new leader and the older (wiser) ones unsure about 'all this change'. I don't actually know if it happened this way, but I also imagine children laughing and lots of celebration as all the tribes were called together, each wondering if theirs was the 'chosen' tribe.

Finally, the tribe of Benjamin is selected so now all that remains is to find the elected man within the tribe. The tension mounts as each group is called forward until finally the new king is announced – none other than the tall, dark and handsome Saul, son of Kish!

There are smiles, sighs, relief, clapping and maybe even a few fist-pumps while Samuel calls Saul's name, inviting him to come forward and stand in front of his people as king. But what happens next is… silence. Nothing happens. I imagine Samuel calling Saul again, a bit louder…

Not a thing.

Sighing as he glances toward heaven, Samuel waits… time is standing still… not even a bird squeaks out a tweet… zilch. It's a bit like the end of *The Sound of Music*, when the von Trapp family are announced as the winners of the talent competition… yet they are nowhere to be found. But while the von Trapps were hiding in a convent, Saul was found in a slightly less religious location: among the baggage. I find it ironic that he hid in the baggage; isn't that where we often hide from others… among our own, personal 'baggage'?

Fear was the downfall of Saul, just as it could be for any leader who insists on maintaining control over their lives. You can read more about Saul's fear-based decisions in 1 Samuel 14 where, among other things, his entire army went hungry because he refused to deal with his sin. (As an aside, an insecure leader is more concerned with how the team is perceived than how the team are empowered.)

Continuing to read, we see how Samuel gave instructions from God to have Saul's army kill every person and animal in Amalek, but Saul allowed the fat and healthy animals to be spared. Once again, he was swayed by outer appearance and present benefit over faithful obedience and future reward. Saul builds a monument to himself (another obvious sign of deep insecurity), continuing in his deception, allowing his personal fears to strong-arm him into a monumental failure.

A disobedient choice

A disobedient choice is never justified. Regardless of how right it seems, if it goes against the Word or the nature of God, then that choice is not defendable. How someone may have hurt us or the circumstances surrounding our decision are immaterial: if God says no, then the answer is no. Full stop. He knows the end from the beginning, so trust His love and watch for His grace to make a way where the path seems impossible.

After Saul admitted to his decision, Samuel reminded him of his identity as king over Israel, while also stating the obvious: 'you are little in your own eyes'. Instead of owning his disobedience, Saul blamed the soldiers,

> 'A disobedient choice is never justified.'

saying that they were the ones who had decided to bring back the animals in order to devote them to God. He tried to super-spiritualise his sin, once again refusing to take ownership as the leader.

If we lead in any capacity (parent, business, church, small group, etc), it is important to notice how we handle disappointment, failure and correction. Insecurity deflects responsibility, while identity acknowledges responsibility. Do you find that you are quick to accept responsibility if something goes wrong, or are you quick to put the blame on someone else – a spouse, child, co-worker, boss, the government? Admittedly, insecurity has always been my greatest struggle, so this type of deflection has also been my default whenever my security felt threatened. I would initially look to blame someone else if things went wrong, even if that blame was only heard in my own mind. The Lord has been working with me in this area over the years, so that I now own what is my decision or responsibility without looking for a scapegoat. It is not wrong for a leader to bring correction – good leadership admonishes where needed – but never by humiliating, demeaning or by casting aspersions to take the attention off themselves. Mocking is *always* from the enemy – do not take the bait.

To the end, Saul feared the people. Even though he was king, that fear controlled every decision that he made… including the decision to take his own life (1 Sam. 31:4). It was a sad and unnecessary ending to a life that had the potential to leave a far-reaching, godly legacy, if only he had chosen differently.

Making a change

As a regular contributor to the *Inspiring Women Every Day* Bible reading notes, I once wrote a devotional about Joshua, in which I mentioned the boldness of Joshua in asking the sun to be silent, or as some translations put it, to 'stand still' (Josh. 10:1–14). I love that imagery. It makes me think of a commanding officer who has commanded his troops to silence. I imagine him walking among them, watching as they stand to attention and waiting to hear the words 'at ease' to move again. We carry an authority as believers to influence our future, seeing it become far greater than our past. But that authority will only work if we exercise our right to use it – not if we hide it behind the baggage of fear, doubt and insecurity, or blame God when things are delayed or do not happen as we have prayed.

In short, it is hypocritical to expect the blessing of God when we don't have faith. Our responsibility is to believe and walk by faith, and God's responsibility is to answer according to His Word. Yet so often we talk unbelief and still expect Him to answer with favour. I expound this further in the devotional I wrote:

> 'it is hypocritical to expect the blessing of God when we don't have faith.'

> *As believers in Christ, we have authority to declare healing, blessing, prosperity (wholeness), peace, righteousness and love to a hurting, dying world. How do we begin? By declaring truth over our family, healing over our city and righteousness within our workplace. We must not only believe God can do the impossible, but that He wants to do the impossible, in and through our lives. Walking in assumption is never right, but neither should we wander about in weakness or in fear. We are children of the living God, royal and righteous, created and empowered for good works. Let's be bold... believing the same God who silenced the sun will silence the enemy in our lives. Not out of assumption, but in faith.*[15]

It is time for the Church of Jesus Christ, in the western world, to walk in a new level of boldness and faith – not boasting, but setting a standard for the next generation to build on. Many of us have become so comfortable in our Christianity that there is a sense of immunity from persecution and a belief that 'it can't happen here'. I am not seeking persecution, nor am I prophesying it, but I am saying that we are in a battle for souls and we will be held accountable for our level of obedience – not only obedience to gain our miracle, but obedience to fulfil God's mandate to make disciples of all nations.

Saul was unable to stand against the people because he feared their exclusion more than God's inclusion. He was invited into a legacy-leaving calling, yet his fear of others caused him to fail at the first hurdle and quit at the last one. In a world saturated with social media, we have developed a culture of comparison and an increased fear of exclusion – this is helpful when it highlights acts of prejudice, but dangerous when it perpetuates acceptance by others, in lieu of agreement with God.

Do any of your past choices reflect the attitude of Saul – insecure and afraid to lead? What about your current choices? You know what I am going to say… if we want a different outcome then we have to make a different choice!

As we transition into Part Two, we will discover important biblical principles which we already possess; ones which greatly assist us in making this transition toward an unwavering faith… are you ready?

QUESTIONS

1. Is it time to start writing a new storyline for your life? If so, what will you write?

2. What does living a surrendered life mean to you?

3. Where can you identify with Saul? How would you like to change as a result?

PART TWO

Let's get real

The life of faith

Choosing obedience over comfort

The past does not define your future; it informs it.

My past has been filled with years of insecurity, fear, doubt, discouragement, disappointment, lack and low self-esteem... wow, even typing that list makes me slightly depressed! Truthfully, though, I really have had to do battle to gain freedom from that which has held me back. I've had to refuse to allow the enemy's grip over my past to dictate my future. Though I chose not to give up, I did listen to the lies of the accuser far more than I would have liked, and I still fight to disown some of those lies today.

In comparison, Jesus did not have a discussion, or come to any terms of agreement, with the demonic during His time on earth: once Jesus spoke, the enemy had to obey. Desiring this same level of freedom encourages me to continue growing in faith, learning about my own authority over the adversary. But, I am still human and I have seasons where I wonder if anything will ever really change. During the times when I feel stuck, I like to read about other people who have braved the difficult choices, refusing to give up: the Samaritan woman who left one lifestyle for another; the prostitute who was set free; the widow's jars filled with oil to preserve her future; the dry bones that lived; the Red Sea Moses faced; the manna that stopped; the blind eyes who could see; the lame who could walk; the outcast who was invited in; the bread that multiplied; the thief who repented; and the tomb that is empty. Nothing – absolutely nothing – is impossible for our God!

It is time we use our past to our advantage, not hide it out of shame or regret. We can choose to allow what has been to propel us toward what could be. We have all made mistakes and faced trials – all of us – but the worst decision we can make today is allowing our past mistakes to direct our future decisions. Choosing to cling on to regret, instead of embracing freedom, is like receiving a brand-new car but choosing to walk everywhere… and then blaming the dealership for a faulty vehicle. Use what you have been given!

'the worst decision we can make today is allowing our past mistakes to direct our future decisions.'

In the last chapter we studied Saul, who refused to make a different choice, allowing the enemy to influence his decisions and eventually steal his authority. As we begin Part Two, let's look at another man who also faced difficult choices, but one who chose to write a new legacy for his family line – a legacy that still impacts us today.

To settle or not to settle?

Terah took Abram his son and Lot the son of Haran, his grandson, and Sarai his daughter-in-law, his son Abram's wife, and they went forth together from Ur of the Chaldeans to go into the land of Canaan, but when they came to Haran, they settled

**there. The days of Terah were 205 years, and Terah
died in Haran.**

Genesis 11:31–32

Abraham's father settled, but Abraham moved on. One of the
biggest differences between Abraham and Saul, or between a
person of faith and one of fear, is whether or not they settle. I am
not saying that we are all created for wanderlust, but Terah set out
for Canaan and settled in Haran, dying where he did not belong.
There are seasons of rest in our lives, and those are necessary and
good, but if we allow rest to become stagnancy, we are in danger
of becoming too comfortable to move on.

When I was a little girl, I remember sitting on my dad's
lap listening to him sing to me, and my mom would walk in
announcing that it was time for bed... and 'suddenly' I was asleep.
A tiny smile would lift the corners of my mouth as I heard my dad
say, 'Oh no, Mom, looks like Jenny is asleep... I guess I'll have
to carry her upstairs to bed.' My plan worked! He would carry
me up and tuck me in because I was too settled to move from the
safety of his lap. Some evenings I would just happen to wake up
as soon as I hit the bed, sneaking in a few extra special moments
with my father as we exchanged 'eskimo kisses' and he sang
Edelweiss to me. But there were also evenings when I was made
to walk up the stairs myself, or was denied the extra time, because
Dad knew I was stalling and needed my rest (or he needed his!).

It is the same with our heavenly Father. During some seasons,
the Father may ask you to leave what feels safe to you, but there
is always a reason. He is still nearby, watching over you, knowing
that your growth requires stepping out of what is comfortable –

because the longer we settle spiritually, the less likely we'll walk obediently. Remember Saul hiding in the baggage? Though he was king, he had settled into an identity of 'weak' and not 'equipped', so when he was asked to step up, the only thing he knew how to do was sit down.

Has God asked you to step up spiritually, emotionally or physically? Is the Holy Spirit prompting you to forgive, mature or upgrade in an area that makes you uncomfortable? Resting in our Father's arms is important, and being carried is for a season, but if I was still asking my dad to carry me to bed at this age, something would be seriously wrong!

Maturity will eventually ask us to adjust our position – if we refuse to obey we may turn a comfort zone into a ceiling, or, as we will see below, create an idol instead of an altar.

Altar or idol?

Another stark contrast between Abraham and Saul is seen in what they built during their lives. In 1 Samuel 13, we read about the Philistines assembling to fight against Israel, and Saul burning an offering out of fear, not obedience. You might remember that Samuel had told him not to do anything until he arrived, but Samuel's delay in showing up triggered Saul's disobedient decision to give up (1 Sam. 10:8). How many times have we given up our faith and stopped believing for a miracle because we felt God was too late and the situation now looked impossible? 'Late' is never 'impossible' to a God who is outside of time.

As a result of his disobedience, the kingdom was taken from

Saul, and God sought a leader who was a man after His own heart: the future King David. One would think Saul had learned

> '"Late" is never "impossible" to a God who is outside of time.'

his lesson by now, but, as we have seen, a few chapters later Saul not only refused to kill the animals as instructed, but he built a monument to himself – cementing his rebellion and sealing his fate. Imagine how differently the story might have turned out if Saul had only waited. If God seems delayed on a promise in your life, ask Him if there is anything you need to do, but if heaven is silent then continue obeying the most recent guidance. Always remember… God's timing is stunning.

In contrast to Saul we see the Lord Himself appearing to Abram (Abraham), declaring that Abram would be the father of all nations, yet Abram immediately took attention off himself and placed it back where it belonged – on the Lord. We read in Genesis 12:7, 'Then the LORD appeared to Abram and said, "To your offspring I will give this land." So he built there an altar to

> 'God's timing is stunning.'

the LORD, who had appeared to him.' Humility builds altars, not idols.

Saul could have learned a lesson in humility from Abram, but instead he chose to celebrate his own power rather than God's

providence. One of the most dangerous, faith-destroying choices we can make is to walk in pride and take credit for the favour of God in our lives. The Bible says *every* good and perfect gift is from above (James 1:17). Not only that, it is wise for us to give Him glory, because if we begin taking credit we will eventually take ownership, and what we own we must maintain.

But if God brings the blessing, He will sustain the journey, as long as we trust the process.

Let go of limitations

Are there any beliefs that you currently hold, about yourself or God, which are holding you back? What about thoughts that are stopping you from wholeheartedly stepping out in obedience, trusting Him for the 'above and beyond' in your life? As hard as this may be to hear, it is nearly always our own limiting belief systems that hold us back in life – not other people, our past or even the enemy. Repeatedly making excuses for our behaviour, life's circumstances or how we are being treated is like playing for the wrong side and scoring against ourselves.

Let's remind ourselves of a few truths about the enemy: he works through people (Eph. 6:12), can never outrun his past, and will always be positioned in defeat. By partnering with him we imitate his destiny – limited, stuck and lost. Thankfully, our limiting beliefs here on earth don't stop God's desires in heaven.

Limiting beliefs are not only found in the Old Testament, like with Saul, but are prevalent in the New Testament as well. The Pharisees would not believe that Jesus was the Saviour, and it stopped them from seeing the fulfilment of prophecies they had been studying for hundreds of years. Limiting beliefs can shut out the promises of God when we do not see answers happen in the way we were expecting. Because the Pharisees expected a king, they could not receive a baby. The answer was in front of them the whole time Jesus was alive, but pride refused to accept what required humility to receive. I would encourage you to pause for a moment and ask God if there are any limiting beliefs keeping you from receiving what He has in store for you?

There have been numerous times in my life when I felt that God was punishing me because the open door looked like demotion, taking me in the opposite direction of my dreams and desires. Saying 'yes' seemed the most foolish thing in the world, especially if I wanted to financially get ahead in this world and have the security we all crave. As I have already mentioned, I am not against financial security – that is wisdom – but I am not a fan of disobedience – that is foolishness. Each time a door opened that I did not understand, but knew to be God, I had to humble myself before the Lord and trust Him by faith, instead of choosing what seemed the obvious path to tread.

Perhaps it's time for you to start imagining again… not based on your past, your gifts, your bank statement or your circumstances, but on a God who cannot wait to open doors of blessing, surprise and favour in your life? You are not alone – I also struggle in this area – so I am asking the Holy Spirit to reveal areas where I am limiting God, due to past failure, making me 'future afraid'.

'If God can do beyond what we can imagine… how far-reaching can you imagine?'

If God can do beyond what we can imagine (Eph. 3:20), then that suggests to me that He invites us to 'out-imagine' Him… how far-reaching can you imagine?

A boy with a dream

All of us have something that has the potential to limit our growth – history, lack, failures, education (or lack thereof), where we were born, abuse, bullying, fear, etc. As I mentioned, allowing the past to define my future has been one of the most challenging limiting beliefs that I have had to overcome. I was never the brightest in my class, the prettiest or the most gifted. From a very young age there was a dream in my heart to make a difference and leave an impact in this world… I felt *compelled* to do this, and could not understand why, until I became a Christian and God began unfolding His purpose for my life. I audibly heard the Lord call me into full-time ministry in 1991, but what did that mean? I felt completely inept and unworthy, yet several times in those early days He gave me this scripture:

> **Before I formed you in the womb I knew you,**
> **and before you were born I consecrated you;**
> **I appointed you a prophet to the nations.**
> *Jeremiah 1:4–5*

I always sympathised with Jeremiah – *I don't know how to speak, Lord!* Asking a girl who was terrified to speak one-on-one to prepare for speaking to the nations… well, it took several years for me to believe that!

There are still many dreams unfulfilled and personal desires sitting on a shelf gathering dust, but I refuse to let what has not happened stop me from celebrating what has happened. As you will see in the powerful story below, the only real limitations on our lives are the ones that we render upon ourselves.

Not long ago, I watched *The Boy Who Harnessed the Wind*, a film about a boy called William Kamkwamba, who lived in Malawi and was raised in a poor family of farmers. A drought hit the area and riots broke out due to lack of food. William had an insatiable desire to learn, though he had been kicked out of school because of his family's inability to pay the school fees. So he blackmailed a teacher into allowing him access to the school library, where he had started learning about windmills and how they can supply water. The film eventually shows this uneducated young boy teaching himself to build a working windmill, finding the materials on a scrapheap and saving a village... because he refused to be limited by circumstances, people or lack of education. If a young, uneducated boy in a poor, African village can learn how to build a wind turbine out of an old bicycle and litter from the scrapyard, then what excuses are keeping us from taking a risk and pursuing our dreams?

A Saul mindset hides away and bemoans his limitations, looking for others to take him where he needs to go and letting them fight battles on his behalf. But the mindset of Abraham follows obediently where God leads, worships Him before the answer has arrived, and believes what has never been seen, or done, before. I know which legacy I want describing my life – how about you?

'what excuses are keeping us from taking a risk and pursuing our dreams?'

THE LIFE OF FAITH

QUESTIONS

1. How can your past mistakes or regrets bring about something good for your future?

2. What would having the faith of Abraham look like for you in this season?

3. If you could see one impossible dream come true, what would it be? Are you willing to write this vision and run towards it?

Highly favoured

Choosing favour over fear

Throughout the coming ages we will be the visible display of the infinite riches of his grace and kindness, which was showered upon us in Jesus Christ.

Ephesians 2:7, TPT

It is helpful to remember that God is trying to get things to us, not keep them from us. For many years I believed that God was on His throne, watching to see if I would mess up, and if I was reasonably holy – and then He might throw a blessing my way. But if my behaviour took a turn for the worse, then blessings would be withheld until I had earned the right to have them again. Can you relate to this? The thing is, this description of God's ways could not be further from the truth of His love. Sadly, it has taken me 50 years to gain any semblance of revelation in this area. I am learning that He is not an angry God waiting to withhold, but a loving God desiring to bless – and to bless beyond anything we could dream or imagine. As revelation of this truth began to dawn in my spirit, it created a hunger to consciously seek God's blessings in my life, and then not only seek, but *expect* blessings and favour… and it is happening!

'He is not an angry God waiting to withhold, but a loving God desiring to bless'

This truth not only changed how I saw God, but it changed my circumstances and definitely affected how I approached God in prayer. I still have much to learn, but knowing that I continually walk under the favour of God has been eye opening, faith developing and life changing.

The struggle is real

Have you ever wondered why so many people struggle to receive the favour and blessings of God, or at least struggle to ask for them? Being an American by birth, I suspect that I struggle slightly less than my fellow Brits here in England because, for many of them, to *expect* favour is a cultural taboo right up there with jumping the queue or putting the cream and the jam on the scone in the 'wrong' order. For many people, believing that favour is our inheritance would be presumptuous – residing more comfortably in the arena of working for favour, not receiving it by grace. But grace is what we have been given, and the longer we ignore this truth, the less we may perceive its gift.

We did not earn our salvation. I think most people agree on that point. It was a gift given to us through the blood of Jesus Christ and we have done absolutely nothing to merit His lavish gift of eternal freedom. So, if we agree that we have not earned our salvation, then why do we feel that we need to earn, or do not have a right to expect, our healing, blessing, provision or any other gift won for us at the cross? Yes, the Bible says that 'faith without works is dead' (see James 2:14), and that is absolutely true. We cannot say that we have faith and yet do nothing to see that faith outworked – any purpose from heaven will require us to walk in a new level of faith and trust. But I do not earn my way into purpose; I walk into it, one choice at a time.

> **My son, do not forget my teaching, but let your heart keep my commandments, for length of days and years of life and peace they will add to you. Let not steadfast love and faithfulness forsake you; bind them round your neck; write them on the tablet of your heart. So you will find favour and good success in the sight of God and man.**
> *Proverbs 3:1–4*

Hunger for truth releases favour because the Bible says that as we seek Him, we will find Him, and where God goes, favour follows. Choosing to put the Word of God first in our lives is one way we can open the door to receive God's favour and blessings. We study the Bible to gain revelation, not to receive blessings – but the favour and blessings are a byproduct of the revelation we gain when we meditate on Bible truths. Similarly, I don't stand in the sun solely to receive Vitamin D, but I cannot avoid this benefit when I do. When we seek revelation, favour will find us: 'Hear instruction and be wise, and do not neglect it. Blessed is the one who listens to me, watching daily at my gates, waiting beside my doors. *For whoever finds me finds life and obtains favour from the* LORD' (Proverbs 8:33–35, emphasis mine).

I know there are people who struggle to read the Bible on a regular basis, but if God has designed the Bible to be our guidebook, love letter, promise-revealer and life compass, then surely He will help us grow in our desire to read it when we are struggling. What good parent would intentionally cook food they know their child despises, potentially limiting their physical wellbeing, development and growth? In the same way, why would a loving, heavenly Father deliberately restrict our spiritual growth? Through many ups and downs of reading the Bible, I have learned that my intentionality to read, even when it feels dry, will eventually produce life and revelation if I refuse to give up. Never let your feelings dictate your time in the Word of God. Proverbs 13:13 is a sobering verse, especially in The Passion Translation, where it says, 'Despise the word, will you? Then you'll pay the price and it won't be pretty! But the one who honors the Father's holy instructions will be rewarded.' God does not set us up for failure. If He can part the Red Sea, then surely He can make the Bible come alive to anyone who asks.

That being said, we all have seasons when reading the Bible feels drier than a day in the desert, so there is no condemnation if you find yourself in that place right now. Realise that it is not forever, and see if you can break the slump by finding a new way to do an old routine. Here are some practical suggestions

'Never let your feelings dictate your time in the Word of God.'

I have found helpful, or have learned from others, to help during those dry seasons:

- Designate a special area in which you do your Bible reading… such as a favourite chair or area of the room, preferably somewhere without a lot of distractions.

- Aim to read the Bible at the same time every day, if possible, to help you stick to it.

- Start small… there is no need to read the Bible in a year! Reading one paragraph, or even one or two verses a day, is fine.

- Choose a different translation. If you have been reading one translation for many years, read the same passage in a few other translations and then note the different ways the passage is interpreted. I recommend The Passion Translation or The Voice as an alternative to read alongside the more traditional versions of the Bible.

- Journal what God speaks to you, or highlights to you, as you are reading.

- Write out a prayer to God based on the passage that you have read.

- If you don't know where to read, find the Proverb for the day and read that (for example, if it is the eighteenth day of the month, then read Proverbs 18).

- Read the Bible out loud and then stop and think about what you have read. Notice what jumped out at you while reading. Do this two or three times for the same passage.

- Listen to the Bible on audio instead of reading it. (YouVersion Bible app is an excellent tool for this.)

- Share the journey with a friend. Read the same chapter or book of the Bible as they do and then meet to discuss what you have learned.

- Slowly read a short passage three or four times, taking time to see what word or words jump out at you as you read, then take time to be still and listen to what the Lord wants to say about the reading.

- Ask yourself what was happening at the time this scripture was written – imagine yourself in that scene smelling, tasting, seeing and experiencing for yourself what the Bible is describing. Notice how you feel toward God as you are reading and what questions you might have had for Him if you were living this out in real time. How can they relate to any situations you are currently facing?

Your words were found, and I ate them, and your words became to me a joy and the delight of my heart, for I am called by your name, O LORD, God of hosts.

Jeremiah 15:16

Charles Spurgeon said, 'The more you read the Bible; and the more you meditate on it, the more you will be astonished with it.'[1] God honours those who seek Him and He rewards those who seek His Word. Please make the Bible a priority – there are treasures to be found in its pages!

We get what we expect

OK, the mentor in me is going to come out now because we are already halfway, so I think it's about time for a challenge! I'd like you to start listening to people's expectations when you are in conversation with them and *notice how many people are expecting something negative*. The results may be surprising.

I have observed that the majority of people I speak to at church, in the supermarket, on the streets, in meetings, etc, are expecting something to go wrong, be wrong, become a challenge or somehow detrimentally impact their world. They will speak about the bad weather, the struggling economy, an annoying politician or their lazy spouse. Negativity is rife, and in this modern information age when there is fatalistic sensory overload, we need to work overtime to live in the opposite spirit. Once you start noticing negativity in others, then I want you to start listening to your own words. Again – what you hear may surprise you.

Let me share a somewhat silly example from my own life. A few years ago, I noticed repeated negative thoughts when it came to reading my post. It may sound ridiculous, but you know the envelopes you receive from the bank or from HMRC which bring a jolt of fear into your heart when you spot them in the pile – or is this just me? I realised that I was *assuming* the envelope held negative news, so I would make it the last envelope I opened, trying to postpone the disappointment for as long as possible. One day I decided enough was enough, and I began changing my expectations. If there was any envelope that looked suspiciously negative, I would declare before opening it (often out loud) my thanks to the Lord for being my provider, watching over me and working all things together for my good. I would assume that the contents of the envelope were good, not bad, and that there was absolutely nothing to worry about. The change was remarkable! Several times since, I have opened a letter that looked less than exciting, only to find an unexpected blessing inside. I am no longer anxious in this area, after wasting years living in fear. Intentionally choosing a different expectation brought real freedom.

I have been doing this in other areas of fear as well. If I am out running when it's dark, and I hear the enemy say, 'You will be attacked', I quickly ask the Holy Spirit if I am OK to keep running. When I hear, 'Yes, you are fine', then I continue on, praising God for His protection, peace and provision. I absolutely refuse to allow fear a louder voice than the peace of God, but the choice is mine alone – not even God will make this choice for me.

Jack Canfield says, 'The first key to success is to take 100% responsibility for your life.'[2] I agree wholeheartedly. Once we become serious about assuming responsibility for change to occur in our lives, then we *will* see change. But as long as we are passively waiting, with a sense of entitlement, for breakthrough to simply happen we will continue in a state of disappointment... eventually landing ourselves in regret, bitterness and resentment.

If I can speak life over my post, and peace over my heart, what are some ways that you can proactively come against fear in your own life? Are you *expecting* good things to happen today? Do you *expect* the favour of God over your finances, family, work and children? What would it look like to anticipate a different outcome for the family get-togethers this year, compared to years past? Or to envision a year of enjoying the team you work with, instead of enduring them? We cannot change other people, but in changing ourselves they will often change. Even if they do not, we still have control over our attitude and response to their behaviour. Some of my favourite verses around the favour, love and blessings of God are found in Romans 8:

> 'We cannot change other people, but in changing ourselves they will often change.'

So, what does all this mean? If God has determined to stand with us, tell me, who then could ever stand against us? For God has proved his love by giving us his greatest treasure, the gift of his Son. And since God freely offered him up as the sacrifice for us all, *he certainly won't withhold from us anything else he has to give.*
Romans 8:31–32, TPT (emphasis mine)

More than enough

As I said at the beginning of the chapter, God is not trying to take from us – He is trying to give to us. God's love and generosity should never be questioned once we have received Jesus as our Lord and Saviour. Tasting the tremendous freedom, grace, peace, joy and love that overwhelm us in Christ, and then questioning God's love for us, would be like the daughter of a millionaire wondering if there will be enough food to eat that day. There is always more than enough!

I love this reminder:

And God is able to make all grace every favor and earthly blessing) come to you in abundance, so that you may always *and* under all circumstances *and* whatever the need be self-sufficient [possessing enough to require no aid or support and furnished in abundance for every good work and charitable donation].

2 Corinthians 9:8, AMPC

There is no lack in that verse! If you are struggling in this area, then I highly recommend you write this verse down and put it somewhere where you will see it several times a day (or better yet, memorise it!). God is not a God of not enough, minimum, poverty, used goods or barely getting by. Nowhere in the Scriptures is heaven described as anything less than glorious, beautiful and abundant. If that is God's home, and our eternal home, then why would He desire anything less for us here on earth?

The tension is that there are Bible-believing, God-loving, Holy Spirit-filled Christians in this world who are living in poverty and lack, not in the abundance we find in heaven. Is their poverty simply a response to their lack of faith? No. Can we increase in blessing (empowered to prosper in all areas of life) if we walk in a greater awareness of faith? Yes. Both truths are in the Bible, and to dismiss one because of the other is to miss the fullness of what faith looks like. Between abundance and truth stands grace.

What about wealth?

'Between abundance and truth stands grace.'

So, what about wealth? Jesus was born in a borrowed manger, not in the king's palace, which shows us that poverty can be our beginning, but it does not have to dictate the rest of the story. Yes, Jesus died on a cross, but the tunic torn from Him was of high quality, and He was buried in a rich man's grave. Jesus also had a treasurer that travelled with Him to oversee the ministry funds. If there was not much money to oversee, then Judas could not have (or would not have) been stealing, because it would have been too obvious when money went missing. There must have been enough that the amounts he stole went unnoticed, because we know Peter would definitely have mentioned it to Jesus!

Jesus also watched a widow give all that she owned into an offering (Mark 12:41–44) and He praised her for it; He didn't stop her or ask others to step in and help in that moment. He saw her faith and I'm convinced that she was remarkably blessed after that day. As we saw in an earlier chapter, when thousands were hungry Jesus multiplied the little, He did not criticise their lack. If I believe that God *wants* me in poverty in order to teach me something then I am believing in a God of lack, not of love. One of the most famous verses in the Bible is John 3:16: 'God so loved the world, that he gave…'. Giving comes from loving. There is simply no lack in God – Jesus never had lack, Abraham (with whom we are grafted into the blessing – see Gal. 3:29) had no lack, and there is no lack in heaven. 'Even the strong and the wealthy grow weak and hungry, but those who passionately pursue the Lord will never lack any good thing' (Psa. 34:10, TPT).

Once again, the difficult question is, how do we reconcile those verses with the fact that there *is* lack in our lives? This is something I have deeply wrestled with for the past few years... and I expect it's a question that will be wrestled and debated until we see Jesus face-to-face. I am not an expert in biblical finance, but I am convinced God's desire is not that we remain in need, despite what I see in my own life or the lives of those who are struggling financially. I choose to trust what I read in the Bible of the actions, thoughts and words of an abundant God.

That being said, I also believe we have seasons of struggle and those seasons are meant to demonstrate the faithfulness of God as we wholeheartedly trust Him when circumstances look impossible. The only way for a muscle to grow stronger is for that muscle to have resistance. We will not know how strong we can become until we see how much we can withstand. Similarly, by refusing to surrender to our circumstances, we create the opportunity for an immovable foundation to be laid – naturally, spiritually and also financially. I have learned that yielding my struggle to the hand of God transforms that same battle into my greatest blessing. His answer does not always come immediately, and my quoting a verse does not automatically move the hand of God – He is not a puppet to be played – but understanding

'We will not know how strong we can become until we see how much we can withstand.'

will happen if I refuse to give up. Once we have experienced revelation in this area, and learned that it is impossible to outgive a lavish God, we are free to relax and enjoy the journey with a profound level of freedom.

No good parent wishes bad things on their child and no good Father wishes heartache on His children. Proverbs 10:22 says, 'The blessing of the LORD makes rich, and he adds no sorrow with it.' The word 'rich' in the Hebrew actually means... rich. God is not opposed to wealth, but He can be opposed to how we manage the resources we have. Again, I think The Passion Translation of this verse explains it well: 'True enrichment comes from the blessing of the Lord, with rest and contentment in knowing that it all comes from him'.

Wealth and riches are not an issue with God, but they can become a stumbling block for us. We need to make sure we don't put all our trust or security in them, because at any moment they can be gone. Keeping wealth in the right place – and recognising that wealth is not simply a synonym for finance – is vitally important. Our contentment is not found in our bank balance, but in our rest, and true rest can only be found in the Lord. So yes, believe for favour, ask for favour, look for favour and expect favour... but never allow the pursuit of favour to override your pursuit of God.

> 'never allow the pursuit of favour to override your pursuit of God.'

All-sufficient one

> **Satan retorted, 'So do you think Job does all that out of the sheer goodness of his heart? Why, no one ever had it so good! You pamper him like a pet, make sure nothing bad ever happens to him or his family or his possessions, bless everything he does—he can't lose!'**
>
> *Job 1:10,* The Message

Remembering that pain is still a fact of life, even when living under God's favour, is important for biblical freedom. One of my favourite names of God is *El Shaddai*, which means 'God All-Sufficient'. This name is used in the book of Job more than any other book of the Bible… one source cited it being used 31 times in a book that only has 42 chapters! That's nearly one mention of God being sufficient for every chapter of a book which is rife with devastation, heartache, grief, lack and struggle.

God wants us to know that even in the midst of that pain, when we have lost everything, He is still there as our sufficient one, providing all we need to survive the season. As we have learned, revelation of His love develops a secure identity which, in turn, allows us to freely receive all the glorious riches, blessing and favour He died to give us. Job had an understanding of that security and love, despite the horrific trials he endured; therefore, he did not despise God in the devastation, but he endured until the end. That's why I smile when I read Job 42:12: 'And the LORD blessed the latter days of Job more than his beginning.' God always has the final word.

Let's finish this chapter by reminding ourselves of the Father's great love and favour for each one of His children. Meditate on these words, allowing their truth to sow peace where hurt has sown fear:

> 'God always has the final word.'

So now I live with the confidence that there is nothing in the universe with the power to separate us from God's love. I'm convinced that his love will triumph over death, life's troubles, fallen angels, or dark rulers in the heavens. There is nothing in our present or future circumstances that can weaken his love. There is no power above us or beneath us—no power that could ever be found in the universe that can distance us from God's passionate love, which is lavished upon us through our Lord Jesus, the Anointed One!

Romans 8:38–39, TPT

The Spirit of the Lord [is] upon Me, because He has anointed Me [the Anointed One, the Messiah] to preach the good news (the Gospel) to the poor; He has sent Me to announce release to the captives and recovery of sight to the blind, to send forth as delivered those who are oppressed [who are downtrodden, bruised, crushed, and broken down by calamity], To proclaim the accepted *and* acceptable year of the Lord [the day when salvation and the *free favors of God profusely abound].

Luke 4:18–19, AMPC (second emphasis mine)

QUESTIONS

1. Do you feel that you struggle to receive God's favour and blessings?

2. Choose one routine to change in your devotional time and do this consistently for one month. Then, answer this: What have you discovered about God through this exercise?

3. What does living a wealthy life mean to you?

Tough choices

Choosing the tough path, not the easy road

What's the most difficult choice you've ever had to make? Perhaps it was choosing to end a relationship with someone you loved but it just wasn't healthy; or staying at home to support your family when you wanted to work... or going to work when you wanted to stay at home? Perhaps you knew you had to leave a job despite wanting to stay. You may have chosen to work on your marriage though it might have seemed easier to walk away. Perhaps you've chosen to forgive when what happened felt unforgivable.

Looking back I realise that many of my most difficult choices have involved or impacted other people. This knowledge made choosing that much more challenging, especially when I knew that my choice meant someone might be hurt, or I might be misunderstood due to wrong judgments. One of the toughest sentences that I have ever said was one afternoon 17 years ago. I knew that my parents were struggling with my choice to move overseas, and one day I said to them, 'I really want your blessing to move to England, but I have to obey what I feel God is saying and so I will leave, even without your blessing.' I had never said anything like that to my parents since becoming a Christian and it pained me deeply to know that my decision was causing them such heartache. I was the one who had heard the calling from God, not them, and so their journey was, in many ways, more difficult than mine.

Since that time, I have chosen to 'follow the cloud' (obey where I felt God was leading, as Moses did in Exodus 13:21) more times than I can count, with common sense screaming behind me to make a different choice as I leant into His leading. Following the cloud has meant leaving security, comfort, familiarity and provision; it has involved saying no to great opportunities, walking away from good people and closing the door to potential promotion. I have learned that choosing focuses our priorities and highlights our values, which is why deliberating and procrastinating can be so dangerous. Delaying a decision out of fear allows confusion and unrest to invade our head and heart, drowning out the peace which is meant to guide us.

> 'Following the cloud has meant leaving security, comfort, familiarity and provision'

I recently read a book about the faith of Queen Elizabeth II, and the author described the time of King George VI's ascension (the Queen's father) to the throne, brought about by the abdication of his older brother. King Edward VIII's decision to reject his kingship created a knock-on effect which has reverberated throughout the years and generations, mostly influencing the lives of King George VI, the present Queen Elizabeth II and her husband, the Duke of Edinburgh. Choice is powerful. Dangerous. Releasing. One person's choice can cause a domino effect that shakes nations – Rosa Parks being a brilliant example. Her refusal to surrender her seat on the bus to a white man caused a ripple effect which is still impacting people 65 years later. I'm sure she did not wake up that morning expecting to change history, but when the choice presented itself, she was ready. I find it interesting that nobody knows the name of the white man willing to take her seat, but most people know the name of a black woman who stood up for equality. Choice matters – and the brave choice often matters the most.

What do your choices reflect about you? Who is or has been affected by them? Are they leaving the type of legacy that you desire?

Real life choices

While writing this book, I posted on social media asking people two questions: What was your most challenging choice, and where was God in the midst of it? It was both sobering and inspiring to read their stories, all of which highlighted that tough choices most often involve pain *and* promise. I have included some of their responses (mostly unedited) because I want you to hear their own words. Reading their stories might evoke feelings or thoughts about your own story, so I encourage you to pay attention to what the Holy Spirit might be saying to you as you read.

Many responses included family situations such as letting go of their children, forgiving family members, choosing to love the unlovable, leaving abusive relationships… Here are their own words:

> *If there is anything I have learned in the past year or so [it's] that I am not Jesus, I cannot turn people's lives around no matter how much I want to. I will only end up getting hurt in the process.*

It was a horrible experience. I don't think I'd have coped without my faith.

I just worked on the premise that it is less tough than what I was living with, and this isn't the end of my story.

Their courage is evident. The woman who said the last quote had left an abusive relationship. I love that she says, 'this isn't the end of my story'. That is the power of choice right there. We can choose to write another chapter, start a new beginning, merge onto a different road… or we can allow fear to keep us locked in a place we do not want to be.

Making a new choice is not without pain – any change is often painful in one way or another – but it can also be filled with purpose. Like having a baby, running a marathon or writing a book(!), the purpose far outweighs the pain, once you arrive on the other side.

> 'Making a new choice is not without pain'

Occasionally, a choice arrives with regrets. In response to that same social media post, one woman privately shared that she wanted to have another child, but she was afraid to express that to her husband because she knew he did not want any more children. She wrote: 'I will always wonder what [another] child would have been like and how it would have changed us as a family.'

Another brave person shared, 'My toughest decision was having to admit I have a lot of issues and can't control it all and having to give it to God. And admitting I have an eating disorder and having to ask others for help and just praying that God helps me with this addiction.'

We all know what it is to experience regrets in our lives to varying degrees, but failing to bring those regrets to the cross of Christ can become toxic to our growth. I remember sitting in my bedroom as a teenager, making the grand declaration to myself that 'I will never have any regrets – ever'. I thought that if I planned ahead, prepared for every eventuality and worked hard, then I could ensure a life of perfect choices and blissful joy. I was exuberant and my motive was pure, but I was woefully naive! However hard we try, life has seasons of pain, and the lessons learned in those seasons often hitchhike along the highway of disappointment. If that's you – please take that disappointment to the cross of Christ and let Him minister healing to you there.

Thanksgiving

Another way I am learning to handle regret is to maintain a heart of thanksgiving. I cannot change what I did or said (though it's vital to still seek forgiveness where necessary), but I can change how I view my circumstances. For example, seeing what we have instead of what we don't have is a sure sign of spiritual maturity. Immaturity only sees what is missing, while maturity sees what has been gained. Asking the Holy Spirit for His view of the situation

> 'Immaturity only sees what is missing, while maturity sees what has been gained.'

almost always unveils a perspective that we had not previously considered, and that in itself is worthy of our gratitude.

Finally, gratefulness reminds us that we do not need to be in control, that life does not revolve around us, and that our very breath is an unearned gift from a loving Father. Brené Brown sums it up well by saying, 'What separates privilege from entitlement is gratitude.'[3]

So, back to the stories I received in response to my social media question. One grandmother, whose daughter was pregnant, was praying for the child to be a little girl when she heard God ask, 'Do you want a girl or do you want the best?' (Of course, that's not in relation to boys being better than girls, but rather God's plans being better than any of our own.) After wrestling with this for a while, she surrendered to God's best for her family, and now has a grandson she adores and cannot imagine her life without. It is easy to second-guess God and think that we know best because our basic human nature screams, 'I want what I want!'

The risk of not receiving often outweighs the benefit of surrender. We exuberantly sing 'I surrender all', while trusting our income, spouse, home or health to meet our needs. The epiphany occurs when our imagined security has been removed, forcing us to choose an unseen foundation of faith over a firm foundation of finance (or whatever it is that competes for your trust). Can we keep believing even when the road is difficult or uncertain? Unwavering faith says yes.

'Unwavering faith says yes.'

While we may not always agree with another person's choices, we can still maintain love one for another. I realise this next quote may stir up varying emotions and opinions, but please hear the heart behind the words as this took real courage for this brave one to share (edited for length):

Over the years there have been many choices I have had to make… However, the toughest part of my life is not something I share too freely… at the age of about 27 I had to either accept who I was and the feelings I had or keep them hidden and not accept this. The real feelings I had been having since as long as I could recall is that I have same-sex attraction and that I am indeed gay. Having been brought up in a Christian home, taken to church since [I was] born and dedicated to God in my first few months… to accept this reality was not something I could contemplate.

At the age of 40 I came out. I know some would say how I made a 'choice' to be gay. That I totally disagree with. Why would I choose a path that goes against all I have believed and friends I cared for and risk losing family…? My tough decision was to choose to be real to myself or not. I still have many questions but have found many answers along the way.

Jesus was never afraid of the tough questions; in fact, He was often the one asking them. Whether you agree with this person's choice or not, I chose to share it because the pain behind making it is obvious and the bravery behind the vulnerability is undeniable. Some choices – many choices – are deeply painful, without an immediate (or possibly even long-term) benefit, and yet they come crashing into our worlds with so much noise it is impossible to ignore their presence. When ignoring the choice is not an option, walking through the pain becomes our solution. These impossible choices never arrive alone… they show-up carrying a suitcase of unanswered questions. People on the sidelines may have strong opinions or throw out unhelpful platitudes, and even if they have good intentions, their 'input' can cause more harm than good.

Many years ago, I was a Missions Pastor at a large church when one of the church members was involved in a horrendous car accident. He was a father with two daughters in secondary school, and he had been fighting for his life since the moment of impact. I was the pastor on-call when the doctors explained to his wife that the only way to check for brain activity was to turn the machines off, and essentially 'see what happens'. She made the heartbreaking decision to give the go-ahead and I watched as the family held each other tightly, slowly walking behind the thin curtain, possibly for the last time. They did not need to wait long; he immediately went grey, and soon came the infamous sound of a heart monitor flat-lining. He was gone. I will never forget the deep, guttural cries of grief and anguish that passed through the veil… straight into the heart of God.

A few months later, I met this man's widow for lunch and she shared with me about the tremendous grace of God she had been experiencing. She was living with a peace that only God could give – even able to smile and worship in the midst of her pain. This brave woman shared how a few well-meaning Christians were questioning (critiquing) how she chose to grieve and why she was still filled with joy in the midst of such tragedy. Instead of applauding her bravery and supporting her deep love for God, they could only view her choice through their personal filters. They would not have responded to tragedy this way, therefore, surely she must be in denial. They were watching to see if she would have a breakdown once the shock had worn off, but she

'not all choices
are easy choices…
choose anyway.'

never did – her peace was real. Judgment is cruel, and to judge someone's decision or reaction, without encasing it in the love of God, is pharisaical. No, not all choices are easy choices. In fact, they rarely are… choose anyway.

A running theme throughout all the messages I received was the faithfulness of God – faithful in finances, relationships, provision and direction. But this faithfulness was revealed to those who chose to walk by faith, see the good, and remember His promises. These were not messages of self-pity, but of strength. These were men and women empowered by their God to trust, even when the road ahead was dark and the past behind was painful. Faith became the key which bridged the gap between where they were and where God was bringing them. I can't include them all, but let's hear from a few faith-walkers, in their own words:

> *God had brought me to such a place in my life [by learning faith] in advance that what should have been such an impossible year became a year that I look back upon in awe of what He did. Father God is so very good.*

> *[For] the most part God has either opened or closed the door. The wonderful thing is when that is the case you never have any regrets in the decision made because when you look back you can absolutely see it was the right choice.*

[I said,] 'Lord, I'm putting my situation into Your hands. I don't know what to do next. Spirit, lead me...' I took a leap of faith and my loving Father caught me in His hands.

Decision confirmed and as soon as I changed I wished I'd acted in the decision sooner.

So the biggest decision was choosing freedom... being vulnerable about my issues and sticking at it [enrolling in a programme to overcome harmful, life-controlling issues], and it had to be with God. And now I make every decision with Him, because I've tried it on my own and it doesn't work!

The most difficult choices I've had to make haven't been one-off events, but rather to keep making the choice to be obedient to what God has told me to do in hard situations, and to keep making the choice to not give up and keep going regardless of the circumstance and regardless of my thoughts and feelings. On the days when I've tried to make that choice in my own strength it's probably been more likely to end in self-pity, or frustration with myself or the situation.

[My] toughest decision was adopting as a single mum... My lovely special needs little girl has been home three years now... It's been a tough ride with quite a few surgeries and negative news but the Lord has changed me SO much through it all... I love Him more and more.

This is my journey... I overcame fear and I'm so glad that I did.

Dynamite Shunammite

One of my favourite stories is found in 2 Kings 4, where we read about the Shunammite woman. For several years I preached a message called 'The Dynamite Shunammite' based on this incredible woman's faith. We will never know her proper name, but the first description we have of her is as an *ishah gedolah*, which means 'great woman'. Some translators take that to mean a woman of wealth, while others believe it refers to her wisdom. I like to think it means both!

Her home provided hospitality to the prophet Elisha, including an extension built on the roof so that he would have a private area to which he could retire when he was travelling. In response to her kindness, Elisha asked what could be done for her and she politely refused any assistance, instead saying, 'I dwell among my own people [they are sufficient]' (2 Kings 4:13, AMPC). Longing for a child, and yet remaining barren, she had perhaps lost hope long before Elisha's arrival. It is painfully difficult to keep believing, especially for something this personal, when you are reminded monthly of what has not come to pass. Trust me, I have lived this journey and I know the depth of pain. I have also learned that if we are not careful, time and disappointment can become a crust over our faith, lulling us into an acceptance of what we have, instead of a belief in what could be. Even the strongest of Christians have times when they feel that believing is too painful, and I think the Shunammite woman had reached that place.

But as we see in the story of Abraham and Sarah, infertility is no obstacle for God. Therefore, Elisha boldly prayed for her to be with child, and her response to him was, 'No, my lord, O man of God, do not lie to your servant' (2 Kings 4:16). Some think that she was content without children, but I believe this was fear speaking – fear of getting her hopes raised after so many years of waiting. Yet, as Elisha prophesied, she did become pregnant and gave birth to a healthy baby boy. The years went on and everything seemed fine... until the day when her boy was in the field and cried out, 'my head, my head!' (2 Kings 4:19). He was brought to his mother and sat on her knee until he died.

Choice words

Have you ever had a dream, one which you had waited years to experience, ripped out of your hands at a moment's notice? The anguish, confusion, fear and anger must have been raging within the Shunammite woman as she watched everything she had hoped for disappear. That's what makes her response even more remarkable. Laying her dead son on the prophet's bed, she shuts the door behind her, goes to her husband, says nothing about what had just happened to their son(!), and asks for a donkey to be saddled so she could go and see Elisha. When her husband queries her decision, she responds by saying, 'All is well.'

Whether she was speaking to her husband or herself we will never know, but we do know that she chose her words very carefully and refused to verbally speak the death of her son until she was in the company of faith. Even then she was cryptic in what she said, as we see in the following verses:

Then she saddled the donkey and said to her
servant, Ride fast; do not slacken your pace for me
unless I tell you.

So she set out and came to the man of God at
Mount Carmel. When the man of God saw her afar
off, he said to Gehazi his servant, Behold, yonder is
that Shunammite.

Run to meet her and say, Is it well with you? Well
with your husband? Well with the child? And she
answered, It is well.

When she came to the mountain to the man of
God, she clung to his feet. Gehazi came to thrust
her away, but the man of God said, Let her alone,
for her soul is bitter and vexed within her, and the
Lord has hid it from me and has not told me.

Then she said, Did I desire a son of my lord? Did I
not say, Do not deceive me? Then he said to Gehazi,
Gird up your loins and take my staff in your hand
and go lay my staff on the face of the child. If you
meet any man, do not salute him. If he salutes you,
do not answer him.

The mother of the child said, As the Lord lives
and as my soul lives, I will not leave you. And he
arose and followed her.

2 Kings 4:24–30, AMPC

There are a few interesting points to note in that passage. One is
that she never said her son was dead, but she did say enough that
Elisha knew what had happened. When we are facing a challenge,

it is wise to consider what words come out of our mouth, because our heart and mind hears what we say, and respond accordingly. Speaking truth without fear is possible, but only if our hearts are already filled with faith, because out of the heart, the mouth speaks (Matt. 12:34; Prov. 4:23). We can intentionally give God something to work with by refusing fear, unbelief and doubt, but trying to do this in the moment of crisis is next to impossible. A visitor does not typically answer the door; in the same way, if we want faith to answer when trials come knocking, that faith must have ownership before there is need. If we have meditated on fear or the worst case scenario for months (or even years), then our words will automatically expect the worst, not the best. With this in mind, what would flow out of your heart right now if there was a crisis – fear or faith?

Choice actions

Another point to notice from the passage on the previous page is that after choosing her words carefully, the Shunammite woman chose her actions wisely – she stayed with Elisha and did not follow the servant. Elisha was a man of God, so our dynamite Shunammite believed that if the prophet had spoken that she would have a son, she was not settling for anything less than life. There was no blame or anger, but simply a choice to remain next to the man of faith until she saw what she was believing for come to pass. The servant was not enough for her – she wanted the man of God.

This devoted mother inched nearer her miracle when

she carefully and wisely chose her next words – words which immediately reminded Elisha of his own miracle. Let me explain: I believe that on one of his previous visits, Elisha had spoken of the time he told Elijah, 'as your soul lives, I will not leave you' (2 Kings 2:2, AMPC), and the double portion had become his. I believe that because those were similar words this brave woman chose to speak when she needed a miracle, she was reminding Elisha of his miracle as she fought for her own. In essence she was saying, 'Now it's your turn to facilitate the breakthrough.' Elisha listened.

> When Elisha came into the house, he saw the child lying dead on his bed. So he went in and shut the door behind the two of them and prayed to the LORD. Then he went up and lay on the child, putting his mouth on his mouth, his eyes on his eyes, and his hands on his hands. And as he stretched himself upon him, the flesh of the child became warm. Then he got up again and walked once back and forth in the house, and went up and stretched himself upon him. The child sneezed seven times, and the child opened his eyes. Then [Elisha] summoned Gehazi and said, 'Call this Shunammite.' So he called her. And when she came to him, he said, 'Pick up your son.' She came and fell at his feet, bowing to the ground. Then she picked up her son and went out.
>
> *2 Kings 4:32–37*

Choosing legacy

Notice that this woman honoured the prophet before leaving with her living son – esteeming the one whose faith brought life to her child not only once, but twice. Our Shunammite woman now realised that sufficiency without legacy was meaningless. We cannot always choose what happens to us, but our response is always our responsibility. Surrounding ourselves with people of faith, not welcoming doubt into crisis, and remaining in hope when it looks hopeless, are trademarks of this remarkable woman, and attributes of an unwavering, kingdom lifestyle.

Only crisis will reveal whether or not these traits have matured in our lives – traits developed in seasons of training and revealed in seasons of battle. If a strong faith is not developed when circumstances are in our favour, then we will never display peace when faced with the unknown. Making a tough choice is never enviable, but it is inevitable. What are you doing today to prepare for the challenging choice of tomorrow? Do you feel prepared to respond in faith, like the Shunnammite woman?

'our response is always our responsibility.'

We have the life-giving Word of God to declare into dead circumstances, and we have the power-releasing Holy Spirit dwelling within us – the same Spirit that raised Christ Jesus from the dead. Perhaps we've heard that phrase so many times that we are tempted to forget its power… the *same* Holy Spirit that was powerful enough to overcome death, hell and the grave is the *exact* Spirit indwelling all believers today. Jesus chose to walk out of hell, as Lazarus chose to walk out of the grave, and we have the same choice today to walk out of the lies holding us captive to anything less than the prosperous life that Jesus died to give us.

Will there be things which happen that we don't understand and answers to prayer that go differently from what we desire? Of course. But remaining in doubt, disappointment, despair and defensiveness will never pave the way for prosperity and the *sozo*[4] life we have been promised – for ourselves or those coming behind us.

Boldly living in faith is a path few dare to tread. It is not a road of ease and one rarely knows what is around the next corner; but if we refuse to quit we can anticipate an extraordinary life. Not only that, as we thrash our way through the briars and obstacles trying to hinder our journey, we will eventually see that a path has been forged for the next generation – one established in faith and paved by love.

> 'Boldly living in faith is a path few dare to tread.'

We are all in this race together, passing the baton from one era to the next, clearing a path that leads straight to the throne room of grace and the face of our Saviour. Will you make a tough choice, committing to running this race for as long as it takes?

QUESTIONS

1. What has been the most challenging choice you've ever made?

2. When have you seen the power of gratefulness change a situation for you?

3. How do you think you would have responded if you were the Shunammite woman when her son died? What can you learn from her response?

Free to choose

Choosing authenticity over popularity

I recently heard a six-year-old boy named Harry give a testimony about God's faithfulness in his life, and it was one of the most beautiful testimonies I have heard in a long time. His mother shared that it took Harry two hours to write down what he wanted to read – not because it was long, but because Harry doesn't have a left hand (despite being a left-handed writer). At a young age he is still learning how to write with his right hand, which is time-consuming for a little guy who wants to get all his words on paper. But he insisted to his mum that he write it out himself, and so he sat for two long hours to write down what he wanted to share with a group of nearly 500 people. His bravery runs deep on so many levels.

I was going to summarise what he wrote, but then decided to print his own words, so here is his testimony, unedited, in its entirety:

> *I am Harry and I am [six]. This year God has answered some big prayers for me. Our family needed money as daddy had no job. I prayed and money came through our letterbox!*
>
> *I dreamt I went to Bristol Zoo. It was a really good dream. I wanted to go. I asked God and our neighbour gave us a YEAR long ticket!*
>
> *I prayed for Isaac [brother] when he was in hospital and*

God healed him. I have learnt Jesus makes the darkness tremble and He is awesome. 2020 is going to be the best year ever. There are angels coloured like rainbows coming from heaven to snuggle people. The Bible says just believe so I just believe and God does it.

My prayer – Jesus send Your love to the church and people outside as well. Heaven come down, heaven come down, heaven come down. Amen.

The cynic may say it was his imagination seeing the angels and writing about heaven coming down, but the sensitive would see that the Spirit was speaking. The authenticity of a child is beautifully pure, without filters to hide or fears to withhold. We've all laughed when overhearing a child innocently say something that nobody else would dare to say. My niece Dorothy (who recently turned six) has a unique ability to simultaneously critique and charm you, leaving you laughing while she bends social taboos. Here is something her mum, my sister-in-law, posted on social media a couple of years ago:

Scene: driving home from work/daycare
Dorothy: *'Mama, you stink. You should take a shower.'*
Me: *'Dorothy, that's not very kind to say.'*
Dorothy: *'I'm not being mean; I just want you to smell nice.'*
(I swear I don't stink.)

As inappropriate as it might seem to hear such unfiltered authenticity and honesty coming from an adult, there is something beautifully freeing about hearing it from a child. As we mature, filters are applied (at times for good reason), and depending on the culture and society in which we find ourselves, authenticity may take a back seat to propriety. I have wondered if propriety and authenticity can co-exist, or must one bow in deference to the will of the other? Jesus was a rule-breaker sometimes, a law-fulfiller all the time, and the most authentic human who will ever walk the earth – and I think somewhere in there is our answer.

You are amazing

In my book *Unshakeable Confidence*, I tell the story of a blind date in 2006 which taught me an important lesson. That year, much to my chagrin, I felt God leading me to register on a particular dating site. After quite a tedious experience of vetting potential partners, I at last found a guy who appeared somewhat normal and loved Jesus. Winner. He was going to be in my area one weekend and so we agreed to meet; though I wasn't smitten, we actually had a great time! I saw him off at the train station and went home wondering how the story would unfold. Within an hour he called me (promising!), and began saying how much he'd enjoyed our time together (great!), that he had never expected me to be this 'amazing' (was this really happening?)... and that this had made him realise that he wanted to go back to his ex-girlfriend.

> 'Jesus was a rule-breaker sometimes, a law-fulfiller all the time, and the most authentic human who will ever walk the earth'

I was stunned. I have absolutely no recollection of what he said, because all I heard was: 'Amazing isn't good enough.' Whatever 'amazing' I was offering, it apparently wasn't enough to secure me a second date.

Shortly afterwards, God revealed something I have never forgotten: *it took amazing to show my date that he preferred authentic.* You see, he already had an authentic relationship with his ex-girlfriend – he'd just been too nervous to take the plunge and commit. But once he experienced amazing, he realised it didn't hold a candle to genuine.[5]

I have never forgotten that poignant conversation, or the lesson I learnt about the power of being authentically you, especially in a society which is becoming more 'filtered' every year. Everyone now has an opinion, and what might *never* be said face-to-face is freely released through 280 characters on social media, in venomous and insipid sentences that take mere seconds to read but a lifetime to forget. Biblical authenticity is motivated by love and carried by grace, whereas the world's idea of being authentic is often led by selfishness (ie fear) and carried by judgment. Yes, we are to speak the truth in love (Eph. 4:15), but to never forget what Paul challenges us to do:

**I therefore, a prisoner for the Lord, urge you
to walk in a manner worthy of the calling to
which you have been called, with all humility
and gentleness, with patience, bearing with one
another in love, eager to maintain the unity of the
Spirit in the bond of peace.**
Ephesians 4:1–3

Notice how the scriptures outline a foundation for speaking truth: by living a life of humility, gentleness, patience, unity, peace and love. Once those truths are freely operational in our lives, then we are more likely to speak not only the truth, but the truth in love.

Who am I to judge?

Paul's words here close the door on the right to criticise, judge, condemn, belittle or humiliate, and especially not in a manner of sarcasm or jest. Sarcasm is like wrapping a weapon in Christmas paper – it still carries the ability to harm, regardless of how it is packaged. Picture a society devoid of backbiting, criticism, sarcasm and judgment: the media, politicians, and those on social media engaging in non-judgmental, informative conversations, void of strife and negativity. While it seems virtually impossible in today's world, when we walk in authenticity, we give others permission to do the same.

> 'Sarcasm is like wrapping a weapon in Christmas paper – it still carries the ability to harm, regardless of how it is packaged.'

What if everyone chose to speak life over politicians, government, cities, countries and families, even when they disagreed with their policies, methods or choices? I am not saying we ignore justice – absolutely not – but we speak about it in a way that invites dialogue, instead of pouring petrol on an already burning fire. The idea of this may seem absurd and unattainable, but at this point *someone* needs to set the example of how to disagree in a life-giving manner, and I believe that voice should be the Church.

Marianne Williamson says:

Our deepest fear is not that we are inadequate. Our deepest fear is that we are powerful beyond measure. It is our light, not our darkness that most frightens us. We ask ourselves, Who am I to be brilliant, gorgeous, talented, and fabulous? Actually, who are you not to be? You are a child of God. Your playing small does not serve the world. There is nothing enlightened about shrinking so that other people will not feel insecure around you. We are all meant to shine, as children do. We were born to make manifest the glory of God that is within us. It is not just in some of us; it is in everyone and as we let our own light shine, we unconsciously give others permission to do the same. As we are liberated from our own fear, our presence automatically liberates others.[6]

Williamson does not claim to be a Christian and I may not agree with all her writings or philosophy, but I do like the sentiment behind these words. As a child of God, be who you have been created to be, giving others permission to discover their own God-given identity. We are on a journey, and who we are today may not be who we are tomorrow – we are continually growing, learning and changing. We may think that a certain lifestyle, attitude or even fashion sense is 'us', but there must be scope for that to evolve as we change. If we want the freedom to grow then should we not give others room to do the same – including leaders, pastors and family members?

Before you write me a letter, I agree that leadership is held to a higher standard – as it absolutely should be – but why have we appointed ourselves as judge and jury (in place of God) for their motives as well as their actions? Biblically we can judge the fruit of someone's life, but we cannot judge their motives. I am not saying we need to blindly accept behaviours we disagree with, because that negates our own authenticity and leads toward a silent compliance with corruption, but vehement judgment has never produced unity. Is it possible to love a leader we wholly disagree with, or to strategically – without anger and abuse – raise the alarm when we see injustices going unchallenged? The book of Esther shows us this is possible, using prayer, fasting and wisdom (see Esther 4:15–16).

In summary, how do we balance authenticity and judgment? These are huge questions which I am still exploring. I do believe we must never shy away from injustice, but I also believe wisdom does not mimic the same world it exposes. As John reminds us, 'By this all people will know that you are my disciples, if you have love for one another' (John 13:35).

In 2013, when asked by reporters his views on homosexuality, Pope Francis responded (now famously), 'Who am I to judge?'

'wisdom does not mimic the same world it exposes.'

He was simply stating that, in his opinion, judgment belongs to a higher power than himself. Walking in love is not always easy (is it ever?), but it is a biblical mandate which requires that we continually grow in grace. While the Church navigates what it looks like to mature in Christ as one body, we are constantly learning that love is far more effective than judgment. God sees who people were created to be, not who they currently are – can we do the same?

Seeing through the eyes of God, rather than the lens of our own conscious or unconscious prejudices, might begin when we consider a child's point of view – a child who sees rainbow angels simply wanting to 'snuggle' us.

'God sees who people were created to be, not who they currently are'

The power of speech

A victim mindset cannot walk victoriously or in biblical authenticity. Belittling and thinking less of ourselves, criticising others, and allowing self-pity a seat at the table will never advance our confidence or increase our influence. If any of these things particularly resonate with you, let today be your day of change. Why not decide that it stops now? The next generation are watching, and they need to witness authenticity mixed with wisdom, and truth mixed with kindness – and right now we hold the keys to this turnaround.

Have you ever been in a mood you were not enjoying, but felt helpless to alter? Perhaps it felt like a dark cloud overshadowed you, following you wherever you walked, stopping you from taking action? Ironically, the only way to blow away shadows of indecision is to instigate a new choice, often by using our voice. (I am not referring to a clinical depression; I recognise there are times we need medical or psychological help to break free of the darkness and there is no shame in that – please speak to someone and receive the help available.) Not long ago I experienced a 'dark cloud' of sorts, and I learned a good lesson through its presence. I was struggling because I saw others living a life that I had dreamed of for years, wondering if that would ever be my experience, battling lies telling me that I had 'wasted my life'. I imagined regret standing at the finish line, waiting to vigorously shake my hand as I crossed it – it was not a pleasant scene. To clarify, I was not depressed, I was sad. Going through the motions, I continued declaring scriptural truths over my life, I exercised daily, ate healthily, guarded my thoughts, and I watched my words... but still I could not shake the sense of despair that felt more real to me than what I knew the Bible said was true about my life.

Then came a day when I had heard one lie too many, and I suddenly felt an overwhelming righteous anger rising up inside. I began to pray loudly, telling the enemy exactly where he could go and reasserting my position as a royal child of the most high God. I declared I was a woman of purpose, deeply loved by my Father in heaven and sincerely wanted by my family and friends here on earth. As I spoke truth into the atmosphere (notice that I did not just *think* it... I had been doing that without any success for a few days), something shifted, the darkness fled, the paralysing feeling dissipated and the air finally felt free again. At that moment I wished I had chosen to speak my truth several days before – authority establishes atmosphere, and I had spent far too long in an atmospheric fog of the evil one.

A few of the enemy's greatest lies are 'It won't work', 'Declaring out loud doesn't change anything', 'You look foolish saying that', 'Nobody cares', 'It's too late', 'Nothing will ever change'... he puts these thoughts on repeat, pushes play, and leaves us alone to fight imaginations without weapons, destined to defeat, until the moment that we wake up to the power within us. As we saw at the beginning of this book, revelation of this power and authority allows us to defeat what is, in reality, powerless.

Once we make that non-negotiable decision to be led by our spiritual authority and identity, rather than our feelings, then other actions will fall into place. But as long as we let our flesh (physical desires, mind, feelings) make our choices, we cannot fully be who Christ called us to be or walk in the freedom He died to give us. It is a battle we will fight until we see Jesus face-to-face, but, as with anything – the stronger the habit, the deeper the imprint, and the wider the impact.

'the stronger the habit, the deeper the imprint, and the wider the impact.'

Living by faith

Early in my Christian walk, I went through a season of feeling guilty if I 'confessed' that I had a cold, was struggling financially or was having a bad day. I misunderstood some biblical teaching, which meant the more I tried to walk by faith, the deeper I found myself in fear. I was afraid that if I did not regularly confess the right words, then perhaps God would not heal me; afraid that if I did not wear a cross around my neck, then maybe I was not showing a good enough witness to people; afraid that I needed to give more money than I could afford or God would not prosper me financially. Fear drove my decision to walk by faith, which caused me to walk in the very manner I was trying to avoid. I'll be honest: even after many years, tears, questions, debates, prayers, Bible reading and soul searching, I still wrestle at times with how to live by faith. What does 'living by faith' actually mean anyway?

Is faith all that is needed to bring about a healing? Does more faith equal more favour? Is it faith that pays my bills and increases me financially? It is a topic which causes emotions to escalate and shame to infiltrate; each of us wondering where we stand on the 'faith-o-meter', most of us feeling that we fall well short of God's desired faith target over our lives. While this is not a book on faith (My book *The Power of a Promise* dives into this topic much further), we cannot walk an unwavering lifestyle without it, because, at its core, an unwavering lifestyle is a faith-based lifestyle. Refusing to give doubt the final word, stepping outside of our comfort zones and mitigating the unexplainable are all keys to this manner of living. Faith is not denying what it sees, it is seeing what cannot be denied.

> 'Faith is not denying what it sees, it is seeing what cannot be denied.'

Non-negotiables

I have several non-negotiables in my life, but these three are probably the most important:

God cannot lie.
The Word of God has final authority in my life.
God is good.

Planting my faith in the truth of those three declarations is what has allowed me to make authentic, bold faith moves – logistically and metaphorically. It has created a life beyond what I would have dreamed or imagined and it has opened doors I never would have expected. I have been in the company of prime ministers and I have held the hands of people with leprosy. I have seen remarkable answers to prayer and I have seen the devastation when prayer is not answered the way we had hoped. Not denying the circumstances, while equally not indulging them, is where I have placed the bridge of my faith. As a bridge it allows me to peer over one side and then walk back to the other; knowing that truth remains somewhere in-between, where answers are not always seen, but grace can always be felt. To me, this is an authentic faith-led lifestyle.

This is seen in Abraham, who we looked at earlier. I am certain he was not overjoyed to walk up the mountain with his son, knowing what had been asked of him. He was under no illusion that, without faith, the blessing he had waited years to receive would be gone in a matter of moments. Equally, he did not dwell on the fear nor give doubt a voice in the matter. He assured his son that the offering would be available when they needed it and he left early in the morning, not allowing delay to overwhelm his imagination with the unknown possibilities about to follow. I don't imagine Abraham got much sleep that night (I wouldn't have!) but if he was anxious over this request from heaven, his actions offered no clues. Instead, as a man of faith, he was unwavering in his commitment to be obedient to the voice of his Father, regardless of

'We will never go wrong giving God the final word.'

how it would have been perceived by his wife or neighbours. I love The Passion Translation of Proverbs 13:13, which says, 'Despise the word, will you? Then you'll pay the price and it won't be pretty! But the one who honors the Father's holy instructions will be rewarded.' We will never go wrong giving God the final word.

Kingdom purpose

An unwavering faith cannot run a strong race if it is consumed with the other competitors – comparing timings or critiquing the course. I ran the London Marathon in 2012 and while I certainly was not keen on some of the areas, and the view was not always to my liking, I did not stop running to complain; I ran the race marked out in front of me until I reached the finish line. The world is looking for *you*, not a replica of anyone else, and when we compare with others, or make decisions solely to be accepted or promoted in the eyes of another, we hinder our own race.

I know missionaries who are currently living in some of the most dangerous parts of the world, but they have more joy and peace than most people living safely in the UK. They have had numerous friends and colleagues killed, counselled innumerable people through grief, seen atrocities nobody should see and endured unspeakable heartache… but you would never know it when speaking to them, because the light and love of Christ literally radiates from their faces and their speech. That, my friends, is kingdom living. It is an unwavering faith achieved by laying down one's life for a greater purpose – a kingdom purpose, not a popular one.

As we move on to Part Three, let's remember our greatest example of that authentic, unwavering faith:

Your attitude should be the kind that was shown by Jesus Christ, who, though he was God, did not demand and cling to his rights as God, but laid aside his mighty power and glory, taking the disguise of a slave and becoming like men. And he humbled himself even further, going so far as actually to die a criminal's death on a cross.
Philippians 2:5–8, TLB

QUESTIONS

1. Do you feel that you live an authentic lifestyle? If not, which areas are a struggle for you and why?

2. What does the following sentence mean to you? 'Faith is not denying what it sees, it is seeing what cannot be denied.'

3. What are the non-negotiables in your faith walk?

PART THREE

Let's respond

Choose to change

Choosing change, not chance

Your life does not get better by chance, it gets better by change.[1]

By now I think we can all agree that if we want something to change, we must choose to change. We cannot hope for a different tomorrow by living the same today, nor can we expect God to simply step in and make everything better without any effort on our part – that is lazy Christianity.

'We cannot hope for a different tomorrow by living the same today'

Making a new choice brings a different outcome, whether it is the food we eat, the thoughts we think or the places we live. We have more control over our outcomes than we think, or perhaps more accurately, like to admit. At times there are extenuating circumstances, such as health challenges physically, mentally or emotionally. I have tremendous empathy for anyone in this situation, because remaining in faith under those circumstances is extremely challenging on a day-to-day basis – if that is you please maintain good self-care and give yourself plenty of grace. I am mainly speaking to the one who has the ability to change, knows what needs to be changed, *wants* to change, yet is not sure how to change. If that is you then this chapter is for you… it is your time to get serious!

Choice is a trade-off

I call heaven and earth to witness against you today, that I have set before you life and death, blessing and curse. Therefore choose life, that you and your offspring may live.

Deuteronomy 30:19

Do not be deceived: God is not mocked, for whatever one sows, that will he also reap. For the one who sows to his own flesh will from the flesh reap corruption, but the one who sows to the Spirit will from the Spirit reap eternal life.

Galatians 6:7–8

Intentional choices create powerful results – positively and negatively. On 11 September 2001 a group of individuals deliberately chose to hijack planes, resulting in thousands of lost lives. More recently, many health care workers put their own safety at risk to help those with Covid-19, saving the lives that they could. Both powerful choices with vastly different long-term results.

'Intentional choices create powerful results – positively and negatively.'

In fact, we all make choices every day that affect us long-term. For example, what we eat significantly affects our energy levels, skin, digestion and life expectancy. The old adage is true, we are what we eat… but we are also a product of many other life choices.

In a 'microwave society' many people are putting their

health at risk by ignoring tomorrow and enjoying today, to their detriment. We cannot, for example, smoke several packs of cigarettes a day and then blame God when we are diagnosed with lung cancer. He did not force us to put those chemicals in our body; we made a choice. Equally, we can make positive choices by exercising and choosing appropriate, healthy foods, but this does not guarantee a disease-free life; it does, however, increase the likelihood of greater health.

In today's society too many of us want benefits without sacrifice, but life does not work that way. As my dad says, 'everything in life is a trade-off' so when we make a choice for one thing, we are automatically dismissing the choice of another. I remember many times as a child getting frustrated with those words because I wanted *both* choices! But they are true. We cannot be single *and* married, or enjoy extended time with our spouse *and* have a newborn, or prioritise our health *and* eat unhealthy portion sizes. One choice negates the other and so then it comes down to priorities – which one is more important or necessary for that season of life? I choose to eat healthily because I want to steward the body that God has given me, therefore I am choosing not to overindulge in certain foods that I know are not good for me in excessive amounts. Or, when I do choose to indulge more than is healthy, I am aware of the effects – it is my choice.

God has created us body, soul (mind, will, emotions) and spirit, and all three are extremely important to maintaining health. When one of these areas is struggling, then often the others will also begin to struggle, but the good news is that we can trust the weak area to the Lord, while intentionally strengthening one of the other two areas. For example, if I am struggling physically then I can deliberately strengthen myself spiritually through worship, or emotionally strengthen myself through prayer, reading an uplifting book or doing an art project.

> 'God has created us body, soul (mind, will, emotions) and spirit'

In this chapter I want to switch gears and share some extremely practical changes – ones which have made an enormous difference in my life and I hope will help in yours as well.

Morning routine

Last year I made one of the best choices I have ever made – I became fiercely intentional about my morning routine. I had listened to enough podcasts and read enough leadership books to know that the morning routine was important and that good habits set us up for a desired future. I wanted to take my routine to another level and see if it made any difference. I was pleasantly surprised!

There are numerous books that present the science behind this theory, but I want to share my story and how I discovered that waking up earlier and focusing on key areas every morning, even when travelling for work or holiday, created a healthy pattern that will last me a lifetime. Another obvious benefit, which I had not realised until I heard someone else mention it, was waking up one hour earlier each morning gains you an additional *15 days* over one year. That is incredible! (Stating the obvious – if you woke up two hours earlier, you would gain an extra *month* of time to spend time with God, exercise, plan out your day, take an online class, etc. Could you use an extra month this year?) But this type of change will only happen if we are intentional and if we stop seeing the clock as the bad guy… friends, the alarm is not the enemy!

If reading this is already causing heart palpitations and a sweat to break out, then start small by going to bed an extra ten or fifteen minutes earlier… making sure that you wake up (and get out of bed!) earlier as well. As this becomes routine, add another fifteen minutes, and before you know it, you will have gained fifteen extra days of quality time which you can use to strengthen yourself spiritually, mentally and physically. It begins with one decision.

Recently I was speaking to a group of young women and I challenged them by asking: 'If you won't make your bed, why should God expand your territory?' There was silence… and then nervous laughter… as they sheepishly looked around at each other, wondering if the speaker was serious. I smiled, but I told them I was not joking – making our bed is one of the best decisions we can make each day. By leaving it unmade we are displaying a lazy attitude which says that we do not care what our home environment looks like… it reflects a slothful mindset. (I must admit that I nearly lost my audience at that point, but to their credit they hung in with me. Please do the same!)

Why is this important? Because clutter… clutters! It clutters the mind and overworks our senses, creating a false sense of comfort, when – if we are really honest – the untidiness is more a representation of laziness than personal style. I looked up the synonyms for clutter and this is a sample of what I found: mess, jumble, heap, disorder, tangle, mishmash, confusion and disarray. These are not words most people want to describe their working or living environments, let alone their minds! I have needed to shake myself out of slothfulness and into self-discipline. I know how freeing it can become.

Self-control is a fruit of the Spirit, so God in His grace has already given us everything we need to walk a disciplined life. As we follow the leading of the Holy Spirit, He will help outwork the fruit already in us. I do not need to go in search of patience – it is in me. It is not necessary to work up joy – it is there. I am not handicapped in the area of love – the fruit is ready and waiting to be nurtured. All of them *already* dwell within me: love, joy, peace, patience, kindness, goodness, faithfulness, gentleness and self-control (see Gal. 5:22–23). But only through my choices will they be developed into fruit that benefits others.

'Self-control is a fruit of the Spirit, so God in His grace has already given us everything we need to walk a disciplined life.'

So, back to the morning routine. For me, I have found there are five key areas that make an enormous difference in my life when I incorporate them into my morning: time with God, exercise, nutrition, teaching and tidiness. When these are in place and regularly practised, then I am able to function at a level much higher than when they are not working in my life. Your list might be different from mine, so let the Holy Spirit guide you in the areas that are most beneficial to the stage of life that you are in right now. Alternatively, this might *not* be a season for you to add in more activity (eg if you have young children) so please follow what the Spirit is saying to you – there are no rules and there is no condemnation.

I encourage you to take some time right now to consider your morning routine and how these practices (or other activities that are a priority to you) can be implemented. To help you with this, I have briefly outlined key points under each of the areas that have had the biggest impact in my life.

Time with God

This is my first priority and when it gets pushed aside out of busyness, or from any other discipline taking the lead, then I notice the effect. We cannot substitute our time with God by anything other than… time with God (although the outworking of this varies from person to person).

I have had seasons where I worshipped most of that time, other seasons where Bible reading was the focus and others when I prayed or meditated more than I read. Currently I am doing a few things in the morning: reading a devotional on Song of Songs, working through some short YouVersion Bible Reading Plans, and daily listening to Lectio365 (a brilliant app to bring focus and help you centre your attention on the Lord). Previously, I have read the Bible in a year or at other times I have chosen a passage to read every day in order to memorise it and get it deep into my spirit. There have been days when I have journalled more than I have prayed or read the Bible, writing down what I felt God was saying – or what I wanted to say to Him. The method is not as important as the moments.

However you choose to spend time with God, make it a priority because everything else pales in comparison to putting Him first in our morning, let alone our lives. (As a caveat, let me reiterate that if you are in a season of life with small children, elderly parents, illness or any other time-consuming and life-altering conditions, there is no pressure to perform or meet an unrealistic expectation. God is a God of grace and

> 'The method is not as important as the moments.'

sometimes our best times with God happen through tears and silence, when we are not *doing* anything.)

Exercise

I have been a runner for over 20 years, but this past year I decided to bring a fresh challenge to my routine. Up to now I have been running a few times a week, but if the weather was rainy or windy (hello, I live in England!) I would often postpone to another day. This past summer I was on holiday with my parents and I wanted to have a morning run, but I was unfamiliar with this area so I felt better if Amber, their Doberman Pinscher, came with me. After the first day I could tell the dog was keen to go again and so it became our routine – every morning Amber and I would run a few miles though the woods, down to the beach and watch the sunrise together.

Arriving back from holiday I was in the habit of running every morning, so I decided to continue our routine by running a few miles, five or six times per week… and several months later

I still follow that system. Something I had done for 20 years was adjusted in two weeks. I will probably change it again in the future, but for this season it feels right to me. What is one small tweak you can make? You can start with a walk around the area where you live, take a Pilates class at the gym, sign up for an exercise retreat[2] or do some strength training exercises. It does not have to be major, any small change will be a good step in the right direction.

Not long ago, I learned another important lesson from this small adjustment. I found myself running outside about 5.30am in the dark, cold and rain wondering what I was doing! Previously I would have never run in the rain, especially on a cold winter's day (I'm not that committed!), so I began pondering what had changed and why I was running in these conditions at ridiculous-o'clock in the morning. I realised that only giving myself one day off per week limited the excuses I could use. If I chose one day not to run, then regardless of what the weather was like the other days, I was going to go outside… so I had better be confident this excuse was worth it! I had learned that excuses fade when priorities change. I discovered that if something was enough of a priority in my life, I would not allow excuses to alter that priority. This is not only true in exercise, but in every area of our lives. If you find yourself regularly fighting excuses in a particular area, maybe you should stop trying to fight the excuse and instead change your priorities.

'excuses fade when priorities change.'

Nutrition

Nutrition is in a similar category as exercise, but it still receives its own heading because what we eat affects our physical body as much, if not more, than our level of exercise. Health coach Nicole DeWard says:

> *The Pareto principle strongly applies to health and wellness. Eighty percent of our results are from nutrition and twenty percent from exercise. Even more, eighty percent is mindset and twenty percent action. While focusing on mindset and nutrition is life changing, getting into action and exercising is necessary for optimal health.*[3]

You cannot have one without the other – mindset and movement. I am learning that proper nutrition has a direct influence on my mindset. For example, sugar can have a negative affect on our mood, decay our teeth, increase joint pain, affect the heart, liver, pancreas and kidneys, increase weight and has even been found to affect impotency.[4] When sugar is consumed early in the morning, by adding it to coffee or sugary cereals, it creates a craving in our bodies for the rest of the day. The saying is especially true for our morning routine: how we start influences how we finish.

Last year I went through a 30-day programme towards healthy living which involved eliminating several foods for 30 days. This was not only to cleanse my system, but also to restart it, setting myself up to make fresh choices. Once the toxins had left and I realised how much better (remarkably better!) I felt, then I could choose to return to my unhealthy nutritional habits, or choose not to. Some I have brought back into my routine, but none to the same extent as previously. Having a new sense of freedom to choose from a clean slate is an amazing feeling.

Teaching

Reading books and listening to podcasts/audiobooks unequivocally leads to personal growth. We are in the age of information so there is simply no excuse not to be growing in any area that we have a desire to grow – spiritually or otherwise. I think one of the greatest benefits, and hindrances, for facilitating that growth is social media. (As an aside, if you do not have a smart phone or watch any television, you can skip this section… but for the rest of us I want to (slightly) step into your business!) Discovering how much time we spend on our phone or watching television, compared to how much time we spend with the Lord, is a good exercise. You might be surprised at the numbers.

I was gobsmacked recently when I looked at the amount of time I spent on my phone[5] – it was (embarrassingly) on average five hours *per day*. That is essentially a part-time job of looking at my phone. I realised that I was wasting many hours, which I would never retrieve, and that was not how I wanted to live (misuse) my life. Therefore, I am becoming extremely intentional in monitoring my time on social media and how often I access my phone. Because, if you are like me, once you open the phone to do a small thing… suddenly ten minutes can quickly be eaten up by distraction. Are we missing the real world by living in a virtual one?

One way I have learned to balance this is by listening to faith-enhancing podcasts while I am exercising, putting on my make-up, cooking dinner, etc. More recently, I began listening to audiobooks while I am exercising in the morning; I can sometimes 'read' an entire book within 72 hours doing this. Audiobooks, podcasts, or listening to the Bible on audio are excellent tools to have playing when you are in the car dropping kids off, going to work or driving to the supermarket. (As an aside, I am also an avid reader of physical books and believe that sitting down to read relieves stress, can help us sleep and enhances us in a way that the digital world cannot.) There is nothing wrong with music or news, but in today's world the news intentionally plants seeds of fear and negativity, as that is how they keep people hooked, and the more negativity we listen to, the more prone to negativity we will become. Music can also be rewarding, so I am not saying to delete your playlists, but I am saying to keep things in balance and think of ways to feed your spirit and your soul during the day, as an alternative to music and news.

> 'Are we missing the real world by living in a virtual one?'

Tidiness

This might seem like a strange focus to have as part of my morning routine, but I believe it is equal in importance to the others above. If I leave the house a mess, the kitchen unclean, the bed unmade and my clothes strewn all over the place, then, as said at the beginning of the chapter, a cluttered house will create a cluttered mind. I am not saying that everything needs to be perfect or that we must live in a show-home, that is not what I mean. But if I come back to a tidy house, or step into a peace-filled and orderly bedroom in the evening, that automatically produces a sense of calm in my heart and mind.

I have also noticed that tidying the kitchen before bed, when I felt too exhausted to do it, has normally taken me less than ten minutes. That is only ten minutes out of an entire 24 hours, but the results of having a clean and organised kitchen to wake up to the next morning are more than worth those few minutes of time. By cleaning the kitchen before bed I set myself up for a sense of order the next morning, and by making my bed in the morning I set myself up for order that evening – if you haven't tried this, please trust me, mentally this might make a big difference to your day!

To further convince and encourage ourselves in this, there is a YouTube clip[6] that has been viewed over half a million times, showing Navy Seal Admiral McRaven explaining to a group of graduating students the importance of making their beds. He says he learned to do it in basic training and that 'If you make your bed every morning you will have accomplished the first task of the day. It will give you a small sense of pride and it will encourage you to do another task, and another… Making your bed will also reinforce the fact that the little things in life matter. If you can't do the little things right, you'll never be able to do the big things right… If you want to change the world, start off by making your bed.'

I love that: If you want to change the world, start by making your bed. Or, remember, my version: *If you won't make your bed, why should God expand your territory?* It is a choice that we can all make, starting the day as we want it to continue. If you are reading this with your bed unmade and your kitchen not clean… maybe those are your first steps toward living an unwavering lifestyle. There is no condemnation, I genuinely believe you can do this, and please share with me your success stories when you do!

Bible authority

Another significant life-changing choice that I have made is giving the Bible final authority in my life – not how I feel, what I see, or the facts surrounding my circumstance. In the Bible, Proverbs 16:9 says, 'The heart of man plans his way, but the LORD establishes his steps.' God is an establisher – one who is intentional and not haphazard. He is not a God of confusion, but of clarity, and yet He is also a God whose thoughts and ways are above ours, meaning that we will never fully figure out His ways or understand this side of heaven why some things happen the way they do. But knowing His Word is true and putting my full faith in that Word has created a foundation which stands regardless of the shifting sands around me. Believing this has not always been easy, but it has been life saving.

Galatians 6:7–8 says, 'Do not be deceived: God is not mocked, for whatever one sows, that will he also reap. For the one who sows to his own flesh will from the flesh reap corruption, but the one who sows to the Spirit will from the Spirit reap eternal life.' Speaking life and choosing my thoughts creates an atmosphere filled with faith, which is good soil for blessing. Doubt, fear, confusion, bitterness, anger and negativity all stem from the flesh and not from the Spirit. If I sow into them, I will reap from them.

Not long ago I saw a post on a social media feed from a well-known worship leader who was responding to confusion across the body of Christ from a young child dying unexpectedly. She said:

> *If faith is really what you live, you may waver and question but you stay near the hem of God, because you have memorised the feel of its fabric in your fingers and you won't let go. If faith is rooted in you, you don't just up and think God changes his mind about stuff you know he didn't really change his mind about. True faith doesn't have time to take a season off because life pain made you too sad to believe. Aged faith has you crazy in love with a good God no matter what!*[7]

Or another way to say it is from a line I heard in a sermon this morning, 'Live by promises, not problems'! What non-negotiable decisions have you made, or would you make, to bring increased order into your life? Are you strong in self-discipline and, if not, what are the biggest hindrances to this fruit of the Spirit being developed?

John Maxwell famously says, 'I believe that the secret of your success is determined by your daily agenda'.[8] He claims that if he spent 24 hours with any person he would be able to determine whether or not they would be a success in life, simply by watching their daily routine. He goes on to say that success does not happen overnight – and neither does failure – but both are a result of numerous decisions made over time. I tend to agree with him, although I think success can be defined in different ways for different people. Still, I believe the underlying principle is correct, our choices matter... and, as we will see, our repeated choices matter most.

QUESTIONS

1. Where are you most intentional in the choices you make: spirit, soul (mind, will, emotions) or body? How can you develop in the other areas?

2. What do you, or what would you like to, include in your morning routine?

3. What scripture(s) could you write out and memorise to help motivate you towards change?

Choose your future

Choosing focus over distraction

The difference between successful people and really successful people is that really successful people say no to almost everything.[9]

Like many others, I am easily distracted. In the age of social media, my distraction level has increased about 500%. Case in point: I started writing this chapter about 20 minutes ago, but only have a few sentences written because the article with the Warren Buffet quote above was also advertising a book I had been thinking of buying; which led me to stop writing and go to Amazon UK; which led me to looking at Audible books to see if they were cheaper; which led me to look at other leadership books in case those were a better value than the one I was currently researching; which led me to consider whether I should join Audible on a monthly basis; which led me to contemplate how I wanted to spend a recent Amazon voucher that I received; which reminded me that my emails have not been working; which led me to try to figure out why my emails were not working; which led me to shutting down my Wi-Fi; which led me to realising I could not check my email without Wi-Fi (duh… writer's brain); which led me to think… I might as well go back to writing the book.

Welcome to my world.

The power of focus

We must never underestimate the power of focus because without focus we cannot move forward – metaphorically, physically or spiritually. Focus shows us the way, it eliminates distraction, refines our choices and narrows our goals. Living a focused lifestyle is also intentional; one does not stumble into a lifestyle of clarity.

'one does not stumble into a lifestyle of clarity.'

Jesus was the king (no pun intended) of focus. He essentially had three years to save all of humankind and so He began his ministry by proclaiming:

> **The Spirit of the Lord is upon me, because he has anointed me to proclaim good news to the poor.**
> **He has sent me to proclaim liberty to the captives and recovering of sight to the blind, to set at liberty those who are oppressed, to proclaim the year of the Lord's favour.**
> *Luke 4:18–19*

His mandate was clear: reach the poor, the captive, the sick and the oppressed, all with the message of freedom and favour. When a Gentile woman asked for help He initially refused her by saying, 'I was sent only to the lost sheep of the house of Israel' (Matt. 15:24). He also said that He would only do what He saw His Father doing (John 5:19) and only say what the Father told Him to say (John 12:49). In other words, He was focused on His mission and only by the direction of heaven would He deter from that mission. Can we say the same about our own lives?

In a recent *Premier Christianity* article I was impacted by the words of missionary Simon Guillebaud who spent many years in war-torn Barundi sharing the gospel, putting his own life in danger and seeing horrific and chilling examples of evil all around him on a regular basis. He says:

> *We're all watching box sets and sacrificing all our time at the altar of Netflix or Amazon Prime, or whatever it is. And I don't want to slip into that. And that's the challenge that I think people just don't see… It's insidious and dangerous. We need to be very awake, very alert… We've got an urgent commission, an urgent mandate. We need to take it very, very seriously, because I know that no one wants to get to the end of their life and be sat there in a recliner with a shrivelled soul, thinking: 'There was loads of stuff I think I just missed, I played it safe, I wasted so much time.'*[10]

Those are words worth meditating on before we continue reading further. Ask yourself: What would you like your soul to be filled with at the end of your life? In what state would you like your mind, will and emotions to be when you have reached the time of stepping over into your heavenly home? Would you like to know all the latest gossip about the Royal family, politicians and celebrities? Or to be caught up on your favourite TV or Netflix programmes? *Or* would you like your mind to be filled with faith, scripture and worship, knowing that you have done your best to share that knowledge with others through creative and unique-to-you projects?

'What would you like your soul to be filled with at the end of your life?'

(If you are able, put the book down and give yourself a few minutes to think of the answers to those questions and whether your current lifestyle supports those answers.)

Focus begins by choosing, and the choice continues through focusing. They are inextricably linked and they create a powerful combination that has the potential to produce long-lasting and legacy-leaving results.

Values and vision

Knowing our values and living by vision are two key factors in leaving a legacy because our values lead our vision and our vision shapes our future. Can you list your top ten values right now, or even your top five? (More help in this to come!) If we do not know our values then how will we know that we are following the right values to shape our lives and future?

In today's world if we are not intentional about our values, someone else's values will shape us by default. We see this happening in society all of the time. There is no doubt that we live in a time of escalated violence, social

'if we are not intentional about our values, someone else's values will shape us by default.'

discord, identity confusion, racial hatred, political divide, climate change, economic unrest and divided communities. We often hear people blaming society, the press, a prime minister or a president but if we want to see a society changed, as Jesus proclaimed in Luke 4, then we must stop looking outside of our *own* ability to see change manifest. The Body of Christ has been empowered by heaven to stand in our authority and righteousness; it is *our* responsibility to walk out that gift of grace… and we are more than able! When we muzzle our values, silence becomes surrender, and we allow ourselves to be led by someone else's agenda.

Brené Brown, well-known research professor, author and speaker, says it like this, 'The findings from the research are clear: We can't live into values that we can't name [and], living into values requires moving from lofty aspirations to specific, observable behaviors.'[11] In her book *Dare to Lead* she has an extensive list of values, some of which are listed here:

Accountability / Achievement / Adventure / Authenticity / Balance / Beauty / Belonging / Caring / Collaboration / Commitment / Community / Compassion / Confidence / Contentment / Contribution / Cooperation / Courage / Creativity / Dignity / Diversity / Environment / Equality / Excellence / Fairness / Faith / Family / Financial stability / Forgiveness / Freedom / Friendship / Fun / Future generations / Generosity / Grace / Gratitude / Growth / Health / Home / Honesty / Hope / Humility / Inclusion / Independence / Integrity / Job security / Joy / Justice / Kindness / Knowledge / Leadership / Learning / Legacy / Leisure / Love / Loyalty / Making a difference / Openness / Optimism / Parenting / Patience / Peace / Perseverance / Personal fulfillment / Recognition / Reliability / Respect / Responsibility / Risk -taking / Safety / Self-discipline / Self-respect / Serenity / Service / Simplicity / Spirituality / Stewardship / Success / Teamwork / Time / Tradition / Travel / Trust / Truth / Uniqueness / Vision / Vulnerability / Well-being / Wholeheartedness / Wisdom[12]

If you have not done this exercise before, or even if you have, I would highly encourage you to look over that list and highlight your top ten values (you can insert your own if it is not listed). Then out of those ten, choose the top five: these are the core values that lead your decisions and activities. (Note: this is not a one-off exercise because our values can change over time, especially as we grow in our relationship with the Lord.) Consider what Brené says above – we must not only know our values, but develop behaviours that *reflect* those values. For example, if I value my relationship with God then I will create space to make time with Him a priority; to say that I value Him but never spend time with Him is a disconnect in behaviour from what I say that I value.

If you find this exercise difficult, try thinking about those things that make you angry, happy, sad, or bring you to action. Which words would cause you to get out of bed in the morning, eager to step into your day? Imagine someone else *not* valuing this word – how does that make you feel? If it causes an unrest or even a righteous anger, then likely that is a high value for you. It is important to remember that the values we say 'no' to are as important as the ones we say 'yes' to, because every no helps define our yes.

Once those values are defined we can more easily focus on the purpose God has set before us, not being tossed by every wave or whim of someone else's vision for our lives.

Not-to-do list

Author, speaker and productivity guru Michael Hyatt speaks about having a 'not-to-do list', which is a list of items that we are no longer going to do because they are not helping our productivity.[13] If we want to increase our capacity, grow in our skills, become more productive or even be available for God to involve us at a greater level, then we must define what inhibits our ability to focus on the most important tasks. Everyday distractions slip into our lives faster than pounds slip onto our waistline at Christmas and we can allow them to become part of our routine or we can kick them to the kerb where they belong. Recognising distractions becomes easier once we have a core set of values, because the distraction is the antithesis to our purpose and that which brings us peace. In the Bible, Colossians 3:15 says that peace is to be our guide, or the 'umpire' as defined in the Amplified Bible, Classic Edition; peace decides what is 'in or out' in our lives and it is a trustworthy source of guidance when we are unsure which way to proceed. Creating a 'not-to-do list' involves reviewing our past year (or month) and seeing which activities have taken time away from our most important values, and then determining how we can limit – or eliminate – those activities from our lives.

In the Bible, some of the greatest examples of focus, values and vision can be found through the lives of Joshua and Caleb. We know them as the only two men from their generation to touch the Promised Land twice – in their youth as spies and in their maturity as leaders.

The LORD spoke to Moses, saying, 'Send men to spy out the land of Canaan, *which I am giving to the people of Israel*. From each tribe of their fathers you shall send a man, every one a chief among them.'

Numbers 13:1–2 (emphasis mine)

You may know the rest of the story – the ten spies said that the men in the land were too large for them to overcome and only Joshua and Caleb believed victory was not only possible, but inevitable. We have seen from Joshua's life that he valued his relationship with God by staying in the tent of meeting (ie God's presence) even longer than Moses, his leader. Therefore when God said He was giving them the land, Joshua believed God over what he saw; his values led his vision… and remained a focus for 40 years.

Therefore, when Joshua finally brought the people into the Promised Land as leader – and they were abruptly met with a wall that did not allow anyone to enter or to leave (see Josh. 6:1) – he was not moved by what he saw. In fact, God did not give him time to be moved by it because in Joshua 6:2 God says 'See, I have given Jericho into your hand, with its king and mighty men of valour.' Joshua was immediately reminded of his values, God's word and God's presence, so there was no doubt that they would enter into the land he had tread upon nearly 40 years earlier.

Once we have a vision of where we are going and what God has promised, unwavering faith proceeds like a racehorse running for the prize – equipped with blinkers and unfazed by

'vision that is from the heart of God always carries legacy.'

distraction. Joshua did not allow the desert to get into his thinking because he was too focused on the land he had already seen. Joshua's faith not only brought his vision to pass, but that faith also influenced future generations, because vision that is from the heart of God always carries legacy.

Dreaming with God

Imagine the stories we might tell if we stopped worrying about what other people thought, threw off those things which were holding us back, and stepped out of the boat onto the waters of faith. I think the reason most of us struggle to dream big is because we have tried that before, and reaped negative consequences as a result. The marriage we thought would be forever – wasn't; the child we had longed for – died; the job we worked so hard to get – didn't last; the health we were determined to maintain – failed. The savings we built up – disappeared. Life is full of disappointments and roadblocks that, if not kept in check, will steal the best of our future.

God has never been caught off guard, nor has an outcome ever surprised Him. Our current challenge does not have Him pacing heaven or Googling for a solution; quite the opposite – our Father is at perfect peace, with Jesus at His side. I find that picture a beautiful and reassuring thought. Regardless of what you are facing while reading these words, God is at peace. He is calm, rested, attentive, and

'God is at peace. He is calm, rested, attentive, and full of love for you.'

full of love for you. He is with you, He will never leave you, and He has an answer to help you walk this unfamiliar path.

As mentioned, one of the most challenging (and brave) things we can do after disappointment is to dream again because hope can feel like an emotion too difficult to navigate; we wonder if our heart can take another wounding and believing for a new outcome does not seem worth the risk. But, we are children of God – and God is the King of dreamers.

The most obvious dreamer in the Bible is Joseph in the Old Testament. He was the boy who dreamed that his family bowed down to him, and after numerous challenges and many years of confusion, he saw his dream come to pass. Another man named Joseph, the earthly father of Jesus, also dreamed and his dreams brought freedom for his family and shelter to his son. Peter had a dream that changed the future of Christianity (Acts 10) and the woman with the issue of blood had a dream that she would be made whole (Mark 5:28). Some of the dreams were given by heaven, and some desired by earth – each one impacting the dreamer, yet also reaching those affected by the dreamer's life.

Another favourite dreamer of mine is blind Bartimaeus who, upon hearing Jesus was walking by, threw off his cloak (which represented he was a beggar) and walked toward his healing. He had been dreaming of this moment for a long time and he knew that an old coat was not necessary for a new season. I get tears in my eyes when I read the conversation between Jesus and Bartimaeus, especially when Jesus asks Bartimaeus what he wanted done for him? It seems an obvious question, but as we saw earlier in John 5, Jesus asked the same question of the man who had been an invalid for 38 years, and who, after all that time, still was not clear on what he wanted (see John 5:7). Ironically, blind Bart was a man of clear vision. He could see exactly what he wanted, which is why, when Jesus asked the question, I imagine his heart began beating faster… he stood a bit taller… his wrinkled, weathered, old face worked up a toothless smile as he lifted his useless blind eyes toward the beautiful, smiling, piercing eyes of the Healer, while he slowly – savouring every moment – boldly declared, 'Rabbi… I want to see'.

He had vision that those trying to silence him lacked – vision for a future lived in the fullness of all he had been created to live. This was the moment he had been waiting for, the one he had seen a hundred times in his mind's eye, and now it was in front of him about to unfold.

That is the way with dreams; often they take years to manifest – causing us to leave them behind in frustration or, if we are patient, see them unfold more beautifully than we could ever imagine. Is there anything you need to 'throw off' today, making room for your dream tomorrow?

QUESTIONS

1. Where do you struggle with distraction the most? What can you do about that?

2. What are your top three values?

3. Where do you need God to open your eyes so you can see with clearer vision, like blind Bartimaus?

Choose your friends

Choosing faith friends,
not many friends

A man of many companions may come to ruin, but there is a friend who sticks closer than a brother.

Proverbs 18:24

The righteous choose their friends carefully, but the way of the wicked leads them astray.

Proverbs 12:26, NIVUK

Do not be deceived: 'Bad company ruins good morals.'

1 Corinthians 15:33

We have all had friendships that shaped us for good and, most likely, we have all had friendships that ended in ways we did not expect. Friendships, like any relationship, change over time, and if we change and grow together, it creates a bond that even distance cannot separate. Moving 4,000 miles away from the US to England was not easy on my friendships, but thankfully there are a few that have weathered that distance and these friends have an extremely special place in my heart because we have had to work at the friendship – intentionally and sacrificially. Recently

I watched an inspiring video clip about a man who donated his kidney to a friend in order to save that friend's life.[14] He did not want anything in return or even any recognition, he only wanted to make a difference. I read that thinking to myself, 'Some friends won't even loan you their car and he is donating a *kidney*… that is a good friend!'

Do you remember your first friend as a child growing up? Are you still in contact with them? I cannot recollect my first real friend (aside from my sister), but I do remember one of my closest friends in secondary school – her name was Darcie. She lived down the road from me and we were inseparable… phoning each other to find out what the other was going to wear to school the next day (we didn't have a uniform), spending hours playing together after school, acting out our home-scripted plays, talking about boys, asking each other questions we were too embarrassed to ask our parents, doing our hair and make-up and dreaming of what life would be like as an adult.

Darcie was not one of the popular kids in school and because I had an inordinate desire to be liked I decided one day to end the friendship. I arrogantly believed she was keeping me from my destiny of being included with the 'in crowd', hurting my reputation, so I became too cool to be her friend anymore. Kids can be so cruel! As it turned out, the popular kids were not all that nice to be around (and I was not cool enough for them anyway) so sheepishly I returned, asking Darcie to be friends again. To my surprise, and relief, she said yes and we remained friends for many years after that, eventually drifting apart due to life changes and house moves.

To be honest, overall I was not a very good friend: I was far too concerned about my public appearance and being accepted by everyone to consider how Darcie felt and to recognise that her loyalty should have meant more than her popularity. Kids can be remarkably fickle… well, let's be honest, fickleness occurs at all ages. But, so does choice.

Faith friends

An unwavering lifestyle makes space for new relationships, living open hearted and open handed. I moved to a new city a few years ago, so this past year I began praying for what I call 'faith friends' – women who will support one another, pray for one another, believe the best in one another and unreservedly live a lifestyle of faith. I was seeking friends who would not encourage me to settle for anything less than God's best, refusing to speak doubt or discouragement or be led by fear or negativity. This is becoming a group of women intent on living a life fully surrendered to what the Word of God says, even when it is in contrast to what their circumstances are screaming; a group where we can pray together, laugh together and even cry together. We have been meeting for several months now and are beginning to see the scaffolding of something special and kingdom impacting, for which I am truly grateful.

It was in the Upper Room, when the followers of Jesus were all together in one place, that the Spirit was poured out (see Acts 2:1). We have been created to live in unity: Adam needed Eve, Paul worked with Barnabas, David fought alongside Jonathan, Boaz redeemed Ruth, the Father is in relationship with the Son and Holy Spirit… relationships matter. And in a world becoming more virtual every day, I believe relationships matter more now than ever. If we are not intentional about building deep, vulnerable, long-lasting connections (including those outside of our spouse and immediate family) we are missing out. I say this as one who needs to be very focused in developing friendships, because, to be honest, I am quite content in my own company! Also, having never been married, I have learned to be strongly independent, which is both positive and negative. It has forced me to find my identity in Christ and not through another person, but spending so many years on my own has also created a natural isolation.

'if we are too busy to have a coffee with someone we genuinely want to meet, we are too busy.'

I am not a relationship expert, by any stretch of the imagination, but I think in today's society it is especially difficult to develop authentic friendships. Many people are already ensconced in their lives running here, there and everywhere; too busy juggling a career and/or family life in a busy world to believe they have time for new friends. Again it's about values and focus. And the truth is that we need one another – if we are too busy to have a coffee with someone we genuinely want to meet, we are too busy.

The power of unity

The friendship of David and Jonathan is too complex for the space we have available, but suffice to say theirs was a bond that could assuredly be termed 'faith friends'. Charles Ellicott's commentary on their friendship says the following, 'Jonathan and David possessed one thing in common—an intense, unswerving belief in the power of Jehovah of Israel to keep and to save all who trusted in Him.'[15]

Isn't that the basis of any strong, faith friendship: the Lord? There was no competition between them, no hierarchy, no concern over vastly different upbringings and financial securities (or lack thereof) and no jealousy or envy. Instead, there was love, generosity, selflessness and servanthood. I am convicting myself as I write these words! How many of us could use those four words to describe our motivation for developing new friendships: love, generosity, selflessness and servanthood? I don't think I am only speaking for myself when, more often than not, I seek a friend because I need a friend, not solely to be a friend. There is nothing wrong with wanting friendship, but if our motivation is purely to fulfil our own need, then we have already started the friendship on a shaky foundation of selfishness.

Another example of surrounding yourself with like-minded faith and unity would be Joshua and Caleb. We do not know much about their personal friendship, but we do know they both saw with the eyes of faith. When the rest of the spies said it was impossible to take the Promised Land because the opposition was too great, Joshua and Caleb said it was impossible to fail because their God was still sovereign. Theirs were the lone voices of truth, and for that reason, as we saw in the last chapter, they were the only two men out of thousands, if not millions, of people to seize the promise and step into the Promised Land.

Finally, as we have mentioned, there were the 120 people

who waited in the Upper Room for a promise, which none of them could have expected would arrive in the manner that it did (Acts 1:4-5)! But the power of faith united them and eventually they shared an experience unique only to them. Yes, the Holy Spirit has been poured out since that time, and will be again, but this was the birthplace of the Christian Church and it happened while they were 'all together in one place'.

Unity carries power and unity in the Spirit carries supernatural power. Are your friends believing for the same things as you? Is their faith spurring you on to believe for greater works from God, miracles, and for the supernatural to show up in your community and homes?

> 'Unity carries power and unity in the Spirit carries supernatural power.'

The Bible says that people will know we are Christians by our love. Jesus' last prayer for the Church in John 17 was permeated with unity. In the following passage, notice how intertwined Jesus is with the Father *and* with us. He continually weaves the narrative between all of us, displaying an interconnectedness that knits a picture of perfect love.

> **When Jesus had spoken these words, he lifted up his eyes to heaven, and said, 'Father, the hour has come; glorify your Son that the Son may glorify you, since you have given him authority over all flesh, to give eternal life to all whom you have given him. And this is eternal life, that they know you the only true God, and Jesus Christ whom you have sent. *I glorified you* on earth, having accomplished the work that**

you gave me to do. And *now, Father, glorify me* in your own presence with the *glory that I had with you* before the world existed. I have manifested your name to *the people whom you gave me* out of the world. *Yours they were, and you gave them to me*, and they have kept your word. Now *they know that everything that you have given me is from you.* For *I have given them the words that you gave me*, and they have received them and have come to know in truth that I came from you; and they have believed that you sent me. *I am praying for them.* I am not praying for the world but for those whom you have given me, for they are yours. *All mine are yours, and yours are mine, and I am glorified in them.* And I am no longer in the world, but they are in the world, and I am coming to you. *Holy Father, keep them in your name, which you have given me, that they may be one, even as we are one.*
John 17:1–11 (emphases mine)

A few verses later we see the reason this is so important to Jesus… to show the world what true unity looks like – love.

The glory that you have given me I have given to them, that they may be one even as we are one, I in them and you in me, that they may become perfectly one, so that the world may know that you sent me and *loved them even as you loved me.*
John 17:22–23 (emphasis mine)

Worldwide transformation

Only when the worldwide Church walks in unity will love begin to manifest in the way heaven desires. We have seen glimpses of this unity, but we have not tasted the fullness. Personally, I believe the tide is turning and soon we will see more Catholics, Protestants, Baptists, Episcopalian, Church of England, non-denominational, etc holding hands across denominational divides and worshipping the living God together. I also believe there are many people in Islamic countries who are discovering the love of God and are experiencing radical transformation as they learn of the true identity of the 'prophet' Jesus, joining us in this vast, beautiful, expansive song of unity.

> 'Only when the worldwide Church walks in unity will love begin to manifest in the way heaven desires.'

A fascinating documentary has shown how Iran has the fastest growing church at the moment, and is mostly led by women.[16] I realise that may disturb some belief systems, but throughout the Bible we see that God never follows the ways of people, and the fruit of discipleship in Iran at this time cannot be denied. The documentary clearly shows that the Iranian church is flourishing underground because of unity, prayer and discipleship. It is not based on programming, fancy buildings or any person's platform… which is as it should be when Jesus Christ is our focus and His commission our compulsion.

With whom are you building the kingdom? Is it time to be more intentional, like Jonathan and David; to see who is speaking your language, like Joshua and Caleb; to cross bridges and spend quality time with those outside your inner circle, like those in the Upper Room? Many personal coaches have said that there are two key influencers to the outcome of our lives – the books we read and the people we hang around. You may have heard the adage: 'Show me your friends and I'll show you your future!' We will not have a future of hope, faith, joy and prosperity (wholeness in all areas) if we hang around with people who are negative, judgmental, greedy, lazy, critical, sarcastic and display a poverty mentality (viewing life through the lens of lack). As much as we may try to be a 'light in the darkness', and we can sustain that for a season, if those are our only friendships, we will not sustain that way of living for very long.

Look around at those closest to you: do you respect and desire to emulate their faith, outlook and choices? If the answer is no, then it is time to consider a new surrounding. I am not saying to do what I did and dump all your friends tomorrow, or to let them know they are no good for you (please do not do this) – that behaviour is reserved for immature primary age students. But if we do not change our circle of influence, we will eventually imitate their behaviour. Equally, now is a good time to honestly evaluate your motives for being a friend… are your friendships more about what you can gain, as opposed to what you can give? Faith friends give and receive – carrying an unwavering love for each other, while championing God's purposes through the ups and downs… as Jesus does with us.

No longer do I call you servants, for the servant does not know what his master is doing; but I have called you friends, for all that I have heard from my Father I have made known to you.
John 15:15

QUESTIONS

1. Who are the 'faith friends' in your life? How are you being a 'faith friend' to someone else?

2. Is there disunity in any of your relationships right now? How might extending forgiveness help here?

3. Are those closest to you influencing you to a greater hunger for God and a strong faith walk?

Choose to be unwavering

Choosing to never stop choosing

> for the righteous falls seven times
> and rises again
> *Proverbs 24:16*

If I heard my dad say 'try, try again' one time, I heard him say it a thousand times. It was a mantra growing up – one that caused me to pout, roll my eyes and pull an attitude. But, I have never forgotten it and, today, self-discipline and perseverance are two of my strongest traits, for which I am eternally grateful. Thanks, Dad!

In many respects, we are a result of our choices: where we are today is a result of the decisions we made yesterday. We may not like to hear that, and I realise there are outstanding factors such as physical challenges, but even with those struggles we still have a choice on how we are going to respond. Am I choosing to eat healthily despite the recent diagnosis?[17] Am I choosing to think on biblical truths and the faithfulness of God when faced with unexpected news? Am I choosing to be generous, even when I have needs of my own? Am I choosing to praise, even in seasons of sorrow? I am not advocating denial,

> 'where we are today is a result of the decisions we made yesterday'

or declarations made from a religious or selfish motive, but I am saying that the power of choice is available from the moment we wake up, until the moment we drift off to sleep.

I once heard someone say, 'Every action you take is like a vote for the type of person you want to become.' *Every* action seemed a bit exaggerated to me, but the longer I meditated on that statement the more I believed it was grounded in truth, because we eventually become what we repeatedly say, do and believe. It will not happen overnight, but if we maintain consistency, and we embrace responsibility, our lives *can* look different from how they are today. Let's finish by examining some practical ways we can make this happen.

The power of preparation

I cannot imagine I have to convince anyone of the power of consistency, because we have all heard illustrations in this area before – whether it be the football player who never gave up their dream of making the team, the tree which eventually fell after another strike of the axe, or the tortoise who finally crossed the finish line… consistency eventually wins. Any good leader will tell you that it is not about being powerful; it is about being persistent. Having said this, there is one key that actually precedes persistence, yet is equally as important, and that is preparation.

Abraham Lincoln is often referenced as saying 'If I had four hours to cut down a tree I'd spend the first two sharpening the ax'.[18] Regardless of what the world says, success in any area will not be sustained without long-term effort and planning –

public exaltation reveals private preparation. Someone can be consistent, but without any preparation the chances of them receiving the results they want are remote, or at the very least their success will take much longer than necessary. For example, I can consistently put money into savings, but if I have no plan and spend it haphazardly then my savings will never grow. On the other hand, if I prepare myself mentally for the goal that I want to achieve, which helps me avoid temptation, the chances of me reaching my savings goal are exponentially greater. It is the same principle with my physical health: preparing myself mentally, by deciding the 'why behind the what' of becoming healthier, helps me avoid the temptations when it becomes difficult (which it will). Winning at consistency is more than doing the same thing repeatedly; it is understanding the motive behind the choice, and that awareness is accentuated through preparation.

I often hear myself saying to people, 'You don't learn to fight on the battlefield.' Once you are out there it is time for action, not for education. If you hope to learn how to shoot a gun in the midst of war, you – and those around you – will die. The education must precede the engagement (preparation must precede persistence). The good news is that we can transfer this concept to any area of our lives, including our faith.

What is your 'why'? What is driving your desire to be unwavering in your faith, health, relationships or finances? If that question cannot be answered with unequivocal clarity, then that is the place to begin.

'you don't learn to fight on the battlefield'

Becoming who you are

Another way to look at this is to think about the type of person you want to become, which takes us back to the first chapter – identity. James Clear, author of the book *Atomic Habits*, said in a recent podcast, 'It's one thing to say I'm the type of person who *wants* this, but it's something very different to say I'm the type of person who *is* this.'[19] He explained that if you change your language you are not pursuing something different, but at that point you are acting in alignment with who you see yourself to be. For example, instead of the goal being that you run a marathon, make the goal that you become a runner. It is about identity… the action will follow the identity.

We can bring this into the kingdom by asking ourselves what it would look like for us to be fully walking in our identity in Christ? Is good health important in the kingdom? Yes, the Bible makes this very clear where it says:

> **Or do you not know that your body is a temple of the Holy Spirit within you, whom you have from God? You are not your own, for you were bought with a price. So glorify God in your body.**
>
> *1 Corinthians 6:19–20*

Is financial stewardship important in the kingdom? Yes, among other scriptures, the Bible says:

> **Honour the LORD with your wealth and with the firstfruits of all your produce; then your barns will**

be filled with plenty, and your vats will be bursting with wine.
Proverbs 3:9–10

What about spending quality time with the Lord on a daily basis? There are numerous scriptures we could read, but the greatest commandment must supersede them all:

And he said to him, 'You shall love the Lord your God with all your heart and with all your soul and with all your mind. This is the great and first commandment. And a second is like it: You shall love your neighbour as yourself. On these two commandments depend all the Law and the Prophets.'
Matthew 22:37–40

I once heard a pastor say that it wasn't necessary to spend time with God *every* day, a few days a week would be good enough. I wanted to ask him if he would be happy eating only a few days every week or speaking to his wife a few times a week until one of them dies. By trying not to become religious this pastor was flirting with a worldly mindset that says my desires supersede God's Word. (Giving him the benefit of the doubt, perhaps he was trying to counter a religious mindset where people felt they had to do devotions out of duty.)

Anyone who has been married more than five minutes knows that there are times you love a person because you are in covenant with them, not because at that moment they are very desirable!

Once we start making decisions based on desire we have stepped onto a very slippery slope that may take us further than we want to go, bringing with it unexpected sorrow, confusion and emptiness. Jentezen Franklin says, 'Too many Christians find that they are malnourished in the Word but well fed on the world, and they live defeated lives as a result.'[20]

We are not aiming for perfection in our health, finances or spiritual walk, there is only one who is perfect, but we should not let the idea of grace tempt us toward relativism and life choices based on self-interest. The preparation we do by consistently putting God first, endeavouring to live healthy and whole lives, choosing faith over fear and being intentional about what we want to see in our future will reap tremendous rewards for us, and for future generations.

If you have not been happy about your choices up to this point, change your choices. The decisions we have made helped shape who and where we are today, so the decisions we continue to make can reshape the outlook of our next week, month or even years. I am currently in the best shape and the most confident in my identity that I have ever been, but it has come as a direct result of small, sacrificial, intentional changes made repeatedly over the past few years. My desire is to inspire you to do the same – spirit, soul and body. The best decision you can make today is to make a decision, any decision, toward a healthier you in each one of these areas. It is never too late and nobody is ever too far gone; it begins with one, small decision.

> 'If you have not been happy about your choices up to this point, change your choices.'

Start small

An unwavering lifestyle will not happen overnight; it is a choice which is made repeatedly until a new habit, and then a new lifestyle, is formed – do not try to change everything at one time. Mother Teresa said, 'Be faithful in small things because it is in them that your strength lies.'[21] Although it's been disputed who said it, I think the following quote is a good bookend to Mother Teresa's quote, 'The secret of getting ahead is getting started. The secret of getting started is breaking your complex overwhelming tasks into small manageable tasks, and then starting on the first one.'[22]

I declare over myself every day, 'I am proactive and quick to make good decisions.' I have said it so many times that whenever I find myself in a dilemma or feeling paralysed with choice, that phrase automatically comes out of my mouth. Once I hear myself say it, then I simply choose *something* and the sense of powerlessness fades. If you struggle to make choices, or find your choices are most often made as a result of not choosing, then start increasing your small choices in harmless areas. For example, at a restaurant be the first person to choose your meal and then stick with it, regardless of what others choose. And remember, it is OK to make a wrong choice. If you have made a mistake, do not wallow over what has been done, but pick yourself up and deliberately make a new choice in a different direction. The more we practise with small choices, the less we fear the big ones, because confidence grows through small steps – babies do not run marathons.

Finding freedom

Here is an important concept to embrace: once we believe change is possible, we will find a way to change. I want to be vulnerable with you at this point. A few years ago I became adamant that my financial status was going to change because I was tired of living with a poverty mindset. (By the way, a millionaire can have a poverty mindset. It is not about how much money you have; it is about your view of money.) For various reasons I had a fear of money – both of having and of not having it – which led me to feel I never had enough, or if I did have money in the bank I would feel guilty that I was not giving enough away. It culminated in a season where I literally had £1.19 in my current account. I was living in a wealthy area of London, walking down the street, when I realised that my account did not hold enough to buy a cup of coffee. I had not just arrived at that place out of foolishness, there were many outside factors involved, but I was there nonetheless and it forced me to look at how I viewed money.

For years I thought there were choices I could not make because of cost, but once I started getting creative (cooking!) I realised that money could be saved in a multitude of ways. It has been a long journey that I am only starting to enjoy, because I am more determined than ever to break free of this cycle and live a prosperous, generous life, which mirrors the kingdom and heart of God.

Why am I saying all of this? Because it began with tiny goals, such as saving £5 per month. I kept thinking that such a small amount was negligible to the big picture but what I did not realise was that every time I set aside £5 I would be developing a habit of saving, intentionally changing a mindset. What started out as £5 per month became a year of eradicating all debt, with the next year remaining debt free while I increased my savings and emergency fund.

Today, I am determined to maintain a lifestyle of no debt, to increase my savings, and to be a generous giver. We can become financially free through an act of our will, but becoming *biblically* financially free requires walking by faith and obedience, as we invite God into our journey. Listen to the experts and follow the wisdom of known financial experts such as Dave Ramsey[23], but also begin to believe for financial increase by faith. Then, in partnership with God, you will have the privilege of using your (His) finances to serve others in generosity. This is when the fun really begins!

The scripture says, 'One gives freely, yet grows all the richer; another withholds what he should give, and only suffers want' (Prov. 11:24). One of the best things we can do when we are waiting for a breakthrough, in any area, is to intentionally bless someone else who is also waiting for that same breakthrough. Give toward someone else's health, finances, relationships, family, etc. It does not have to be financial giving – you could offer to babysit for a new mum, even though you are aching to be a mother yourself; or to pray and fast for someone's healing, as you are waiting on your own.

Using wisdom, living sacrificially, following common sense and being generous are all keys to financial freedom. This is not a book on finances but I do believe it is one of the most important areas of consistency in our walk with God and an unwavering lifestyle because 'where your treasure is, there your heart will be also' (Matt. 6:21).

Good questions

Good choices often begin with asking the right questions. The Bible says, 'Where there is no guidance, a people falls, but in an abundance of counsellors there is safety' (Prov. 11:14). This mostly refers to leadership of a country but we can also apply it to our personal lives. Seeking the Lord intentionally, along with wise counsel, releases the necessary wisdom and direction needed to transition from one place to another. The Bible is filled with wisdom from beginning to end; for example, the book of Proverbs carries a wealth of revelation, while the New Testament reveals so much about living an unwavering life of love.

Last year I read the book *Fasting* by Jentezen Franklin and I was struck by the truths described in Matthew 6 – a chapter addressing giving, praying, fasting and living free from anxiety... all of which require intentional choices. Making good choices is not always easy – in fact, quite the opposite. Just look at Adam and Eve! But unlike them, we have the Bible, history, the indwelling Holy Spirit and one another to help us choose wisely. Even more importantly, we have Jesus – who shows us that freedom comes, not from avoiding a tree, but from embracing a cross. The choice is ours.

QUESTIONS

1. In what ways are you/will you be intentionally preparing to have an unwavering lifestyle?

2. What is your first small change that you will make after reading this book?

3. How can the choices you make in this area impact the lives of others?

I would like to finish with ten practical questions I have previously asked myself when I was facing a difficult decision and I pray they will be helpful in your own journey. Remember, living an unwavering lifestyle means making the tough choices, being brave, fighting fear and *choosing what others are unwilling to choose, in order to live a life others are unwilling to live.*

1. What do my spiritual leaders say?

2. What do my closest friends say?

3. What does my gut say?

4. Is fear leading this decision?

5. Is this in line with God's purposes for my life? (vision/values)

6. If I say 'no' how do I feel?

7. Which answer is outside of my comfort zone?

8. Do I have peace about the timing?

9. Who else will this decision affect and what do they say?

10. Have I fully surrendered my will and the outcome to God?

Epilogue

Success is measuring yourself against other people; excellence is measuring yourself against your own potential. When you choose excellence you move closer to your potential.[1]

I like the distinction in that quote because it summarises an unwavering lifestyle – not aiming for success, but building excellence. Our success is not about how well we compare to others, or how many social media followers we have, but it is about fulfilling the God-given potential that each one of us carries inside.

Jesus is speaking in John 17:4 when He says, 'I glorified you on earth By completing down to the last detail What you assigned me to do' (*The Message*). His focus was on His assignment, full stop. He was not even distracted by the overwhelming needs of others, as seen by the way He initially refused the Canaanite woman whose daughter was demon possessed. His mission was clear, the lost sheep of Israel, and that would not change, even for a child. (Though her faith did eventually move Him to perform a miracle.)

We must not let our circumstances, other people, jealousy, fear, pride or comparison move us to make decisions, because none of those holds enough substance to sustain purpose; but we would be wise to walk in faith and desire a partnership with heaven that sees His will accomplished on earth through our obedience, creating a life beyond anything we could dream or even imagine (see Eph. 3:20).

Who do you want to become this coming year? What passions remain to be fulfilled before you die? It could be the salvation of your family, the feeding of the homeless, the teaching of the Word, the mission field, starting a business, getting involved in your community, volunteering, spending more time with your grandchildren, writing a book, producing a song, selling a painting, running a marathon, seeing blind eyes healed or a multitude of other dreams.

This is your year; this is your time; this is your choice. I believe in you, yet much more importantly, God the Father, Jesus His Son, Holy Spirit and all of heaven are cheering you on!

Keep running your race… the hard choices are always worth making.

See you at the finish line!

Do you not know that in a race all the runners run, but only one receives the prize? So run that you may obtain it. Every athlete exercises self-control in all things. They do it to receive a perishable wreath, but we an imperishable. So I do not run aimlessly; I do not box as one beating the air. But I discipline my body and keep it under control, lest after preaching to others I myself should be disqualified.
1 Corinthians 9:24–27

Author's Notes

We made it! I'm so pleased you joined me on this journey and I pray you have been encouraged, challenged and blessed by our time together. I give God all the glory for how He has blessed my life and I have no greater desire than seeing others walking in victory with Him.

If you have never made Jesus the Lord of your life, or if you would like to rededicate your life to Him, please join me in praying the following prayer:

> **Dear God,**
>
> **I come to You in the name of Jesus. I admit that I have not trusted You to be my Saviour and have tried to live on my own terms. I ask You to forgive me of all my sins. The Bible says if I confess with my mouth that 'Jesus is Lord', and believe in my heart that God raised Him from the dead, I will be saved (Rom. 10:9). I believe with my heart and I confess with my mouth that Jesus is the Lord and Saviour of my life from this moment forward. Thank You for saving me!**
>
> **In Jesus' name, I pray. Amen.**

If you have prayed that prayer, I would love to celebrate with you! Please let me know by emailing your testimony to **jen@jenbaker.co.uk**. Also, please share with a trusted friend and find a strong Bible-teaching, Spirit-filled church to become part of, as we cannot do this journey alone.

Finally, I would love to stay in touch with you through social media. You can find me on Instagram, Facebook and Twitter here: @jenbakerinspire

Other books by Jen Baker:

- Unshakeable Confidence
- Untangled
- Unlimited
- The Power of a Promise
- Face to Face

Acknowledgments

Writing a book is a journey filled with ups, downs, turnarounds, and occasional dead ends. I always find the journey of a book fascinating – from the initial conception, to a written outline, to a general shape as it is typed, and finally a personality as it is edited. There are hundreds of solitude hours between you and the keyboard... leaving space to wonder if anything you are writing will be relatable, trusting the Lord to skim the dross and surface the gold.

Within the solitude always stand the unseen, unknown champions metaphorically holding up the arms of a weary author through their prayers, encouragement, texts, lattes and chocolate. I want to highlight a few of those heroes, giving honour where honour is due... and for anyone I may miss, please accept my honest, sincere apology.

My parents. You always get the first mention because, quite frankly, I wouldn't be here without you. Thank you for loving each other, loving me and giving me my first glimpse at an unwavering lifestyle. I love you... so very much.

Werner/Tammi and Bobby/Kimi. I know that you are always in the background cheering me on – *thank you*.

Dorothy. Thank you for giving me so much material to work with... Auntie Jen loves you so much, please don't ever change. Hobbes, you'll make my next book.

Lisa. You are at the top of the acknowledgments in every book because you are more devoted to Christ and His cause than almost anyone that I know. You are a faithful servant carrying a warrior's heart and I am truly grateful for everything you have done to help facilitate the release of this book. You are the epitome of unwavering in the kingdom.

Faith friends. Thank you for accepting the invitation to step into this journey together. I love you ladies – you are faithful, bold, strong, beautiful, brave, faith-filled, wise, courageous and *unwavering*. Let's do this!

Rachel. Thank you for the chocolate. Like, really…. Thank you.

Judy. Thank you for letting me share a chapter of your story… you are incredible.

My prayer team. Again, thank you for standing in the gap for me while I was writing. I could literally feel the difference when I knew you were praying; I am truly grateful for each and every time you took me before the throne.

Waverley Abbey Resources team. Thank you for all you did to make this project come to life, and a special thank you to Lynette for your unyielding patience and compassion throughout the journey. As always, thank you to Rebecca and Katie for making me sound better than I am. Your eye for detail and gentle correction make the editing process so much more fun!

The reader. This book is for you. My prayer is that as you read, you will feel empowered, emboldened, encouraged and inspired to live your fullest and freest life – a life of unwavering commitment to a kingdom lifestyle. You are uniquely brave, each one of you, and I count it an honour that we can share this time together. Much love in Christ – Jen.

Endnotes

INTRODUCTION

[1] Gary Wiens, *Come to Papa* (Grandview, MO: Oasis House, 2003) p103

PART ONE

[1] Instagram, @shelleygiglio , 10 January 2020

[2] Steve Uppal, *The Burning Ones* (Maidstone: River Publishers and Media Ltd, 2013) p38

[3] Charles Finney, see www.goodreads.com/quotes/450028-prevailing-prayer-is-that-which-secures-an-answer-saying-prayers

[4] Gary Wiens, *Come to Papa*, p21

[5] Coffee with Jen includes one-to-one, group, and online mentoring with Jen. More information can be found at jenbaker.co.uk/coffee-with-jen

[6] Bill Johnson, *Dreaming with God: Co-Laboring with God for Cultural Transformation* (Shippensburg, PA: Destiny Image, 2010) p85

[7] See www.youtube.com/watch?v=bJ8Kq1wucsk

[8] See www.collinsdictionary.com/dictionary/english/entitlement

[9] Jen Baker, *Unshakeable Confidence* (Farnham, Surrey: CWR, 2018) p31

[10] See www.merriam-webster.com/dictionary/abdication

[11] My book *Unshakeable Confidence* is also a helpful book to read for more study in this area.

[12] Brian Simmonds, *The Divine Romance* (Racine, WI: Broadstreet Publishing Group, LLC, 2017) p42

[13] HELPS Word-studies taken from *The Discovery Bible* software, available at thediscoverybible.com, copyright © 2018, HELPS Ministries Inc. Used by permission. All rights reserved.

[14] Reinhard Bonnke, *Evangelism by Fire: Keys for Effectively Reaching Others With the Gospel* (Lake Mary, FL: Charisma House, 2011) p67

[15] My 17 July entry in *Inspiring Women Every Day*, July/August 2019 issue (Farnham, Surrey: CWR, 2019)

PART TWO

1 Charles Spurgeon, *The Complete Works of C.H. Spurgeon* (Harrington, DE: Delmarva Publications Inc, 2013) p1

2 As heard on Terri Savelle Foy podcast, 20 January 2020, '6 Bad Habits to Break in 2020'

3 Brené Brown, www.goodreads.com/quotes/858472-what-separates-privilege-from-entitlement-is-gratitude

4 Strong's #4982: sozo (pronounced sode'-zo) to save, ie deliver or protect (literally or figuratively): heal, preserve, save (self), do well, be (make) whole

5 Based on the story I tell… See my book, *Unshakeable Confidence* (Farnham, Surrey: CWR, 2018) pp67–68

6 From en.wikiquote.org/wiki/Marianne_Williamson

PART THREE

1 Jim Rohn, www.goodreads.com/quotes/561636-your-life-does-not-get-better-by-chance-it-gets

2 FitFish is a non-judgmental, encouraging place to start if you are looking for a balanced retreat which addresses body, soul and spirit. More information at fit-fish.co.uk

3 NASM Master Trainer and C.O.P.E (Center for Obesity Prevention and Education) Certified Health Coach.

4 See www.webmd.com/diabetes/features/how-sugar-affects-your-body

5 Under settings, most phones will have a setting that records how much time you spend on the phone daily and weekly.

6 See www.youtube.com/watch?v=KgzLzbd-zT4

7 Instagram, @ritaspringer 17 December 2019

8 See www.johnmaxwell.com/blog/it-all-comes-down-to-what-you-do-daily/

9 Warren Buffet, www.inc.com/marcel-schwantes/warren-buffett-says-this-is-1-simple-habit-that-separates-successful-people-from-everyone-else.html

10 www.premierchristianity.com/Past-Issues/2020/January-2020/Simon-Guillebaud-Meet-the-missionary-who-faced-death-threats-in-what-was-once-the-world-s-most-dangerous-nation?fbclid=IwAR08Tpe-zILKwEDBckCL33SV-vURu0H8o40pILxjHxRv27D0vtPZcSa4lrcI

11 See daretolead.brenebrown.com/operationalizing-your-orgs-values/

12 Brené Brown, *Dare to Lead* (London: Vermilion, 2018) pp187–188

[13] See michaelhyatt.com/do-you-have-a-not-to-do-list/

[14] See www.organdonation.nhs.uk/helping-you-to-decide/real-life-stories/living-donation-stories/darren-received-a-kidney-from-a-friend/

[15] Commentary on 1 Samuel 18:1, HELPS Word-studies taken from *The Discovery Bible* software, available at thediscoverybible.com, copyright © 2018, HELPS Ministries Inc. Used by permission. All rights reserved.

[16] See www.foxnews.com/faith-values/worlds-fastest-growing-church-women-documentary-film

[17] Always speak to your GP before making any major changes to your diet.

[18] See quoteinvestigator.com/2014/03/29/sharp-axe/

[19] EntreLeadership podcast, #356 How to Build Great Habits with James Clear, 6 January 2020

[20] Jentezen Franklin, *Fasting* (Lake Mary, FL: Charisma House, 2008) p122

[21] See www.goodreads.com/quotes/243949-be-faithful-in-small-things-because-it-is-in-them

[22] See quoteinvestigator.com/2018/02/03/start/

[23] See www.daveramsey.com

EPILOGUE

[1] Tim Tassopoulos in Jeff Henderson, *Know What You're For* Audiobook, Section 4 (Zondervan, 2019)

Notes

Notes

More from Jen Baker

Unshakeable Confidence

Confidence can take many guises, but what does true, unshakeable confidence look like? Guided by the truth and strength of God's Word and the power of His unwavering love for each one of us — and with vulnerable transparency — Jen walks us through her own journey from debilitating fear to unshakeable confidence. Along the way, you'll develop the kind of confidence that will help to silence the voice of doubt and empower you to become the woman that God created you to be.

Untangled (Devotional Journal)

God is good. He has good plans for you. Fear and regrets can often hold us back. Learn how to overcome such challenges by exploring different 'Freedom from' themes and delve into a transformative time with God.

Unlimited (Devotional Journal)

God's love for us is limitless. He wants us to live a life full of purpose, unrestricted by the things that try to lessen our true identity in Jesus. This book is an invitation to journal your own story of a life unlimited.

For more information, current prices and to order visit
waverleyabbeyresources.org

Inspiring Women

Spend quality time with God

Inspiring Women Every Day

Written by women for women, these daily Bible reading notes offer insights that can be applied to your life every day.

To find out more visit

waverleyabbeyresources.org/inspiring-women-every-day

WAVERLEY ABBEY TRUST

We are a charity serving Christians around the world with practical resources and teaching. We support you to grow in your Christian faith, understand the times in which we live, and serve God in every sphere of life.

waverleyabbeycollege.ac.uk

waverleyabbeyresources.org

waverleyabbeyhouse.org